T0377741

The Political Economy of Good Governance

The Political Economy of Good Governance

Sisay Asefa
Wei-Chiao Huang

2015

W.E. Upjohn Institute for Employment Research
Kalamazoo, Michigan

Library of Congress Cataloging-in-Publication Data

The political economy of good governance / Sisay Asefa and Wei-Chiao Huang, editors.
   ISBN 978-0-88099-496-5 (pbk. : alk. paper) — ISBN 0-88099-496-7 (pbk. : alk. paper) — ISBN 978-0-88099-497-2 (hardcover : alk. paper) — ISBN 0-88099-497-5 (hardcover : alk. paper)

2015940597

© 2015
W.E. Upjohn Institute for Employment Research
300 S. Westnedge Avenue
Kalamazoo, Michigan 49007-4686

The facts presented in this study and the observations and viewpoints expressed are the sole responsibility of the authors. They do not necessarily represent positions of the W.E. Upjohn Institute for Employment Research.

Cover design by Alcorn Publication Design.
Index prepared by Diane Worden.
Printed in the United States of America.
Printed on recycled paper.

Contents

Acknowledgments   vii

1   **Introduction**   1
Sisay Asefa and Wei-Chiao Huang

2   **The Role of Performance Management in Good Governance**   15
Carolyn J. Heinrich

3   **Political Parties, Democracy, and "Good Governance"**   35
John Ishiyama

4   **Good Governance in Transition Economies:**   51
A Comparative Analysis
Susan J. Linz

5   **Governance Challenges in Education and Health Care in**   93
Developing Countries
Seema Jayachandran

6   **Governance Problems and Priorities for Local Climate**   111
Adaptation and Poverty Alleviation
Stephen C. Smith

7   **The Challenges of Good Governance and Leadership in**   131
Developing Countries: Cases from Africa and China
Sisay Asefa and Wei-Chiao Huang

Authors   155

Index   157

About the Institute   173

Acknowledgments

The chapters in this book are based on presentations made at the forty-ninth annual Werner Sichel Economics Lecture Series, hosted by the Department of Economics during the 2012–2013 academic year on the campus of Western Michigan University. The series is made possible through the financial support of the W. E. Upjohn Institute for Employment Research and Western Michigan University. It is named for Dr. Werner Sichel, who retired in the spring semester of 2005 following 45 years of teaching and service to the Department of Economics and WMU.

In codirecting this series and preparing this book, we are grateful to our colleagues in the Department of Economics at WMU for their cooperation in organizing and participating in the lecture series.

Finally, we are especially thankful to the W. E. Upjohn Institute for Employment Research for cosponsoring the series and for the excellent editorial services it rendered during the publication of the book. We take full responsibility for our interpretation of views as expressed in the introductory and concluding chapters of the book, which were not part of the Sichel series.

1
Introduction

Sisay Asefa
Wei-Chiao Huang
Western Michigan University

Governance is a multidimensional concept that involves the traditions and institutions under which political authority in a country is exercised. Governance includes the process by which rulers are selected, monitored, and replaced, and it entails the capacity of governments to effectively formulate and implement sound and inclusive policies. Through these means, good governance fosters the ability of a government to earn the respect of its citizens as well as the cooperation of the institutions that determine its economic and social policies, which influence interaction among citizens. Sustainable development requires good governance that is predictable, open, enlightened, accountable, inclusive of all citizens, and operates under the rule of law. Good governance is desirable as a goal in its own right, beyond being an important means of sustainable development. According to the World Bank, good governance involves six aspects: 1) voice and accountability, 2) political stability and the absence of violence, 3) government effectiveness, 4) regulatory quality, 5) rule of law, and 6) control of corruption. The data the World Bank generates for indicators of governance for all countries around the world are available at www.govindicators .org. The criteria the World Bank uses include consideration of the aforementioned processes in good governance (Kaufmann 2010).

CHAPTER HIGHLIGHTS

This introductory chapter outlines the general points of good governance and its challenges, which will be explored in further detail throughout the book. Subsequent chapters consider how governance relates to performance management, the influence of political parties, education and health issues in developing countries, and the effects of climate on poverty. Key examples will be drawn from countries in eastern Europe, Asia, and Africa.

Chapter 2, titled "The Role of Performance Management in Good Governance," comes from Carolyn J. Heinrich, Sid Richardson Professor of Public Affairs and director of the Center for Health and Social Policy at the Lyndon B. Johnson School of Public Affairs, University of Texas at Austin. She defines "governance" as consisting of "regimes of laws, rules, judicial decisions and administrative practices that constrain, prescribe and enable the provision of publicly supported goods and services." Her focus is on performance management originating from public administration and policy.

Heinrich notes that the twenty-first century is an era of governance by performance management. This approach has long roots in economics and business management, with a focus on four issues: 1) performance management, its origin, and how it contributes to good governance; 2) the challenges and complexity of designing appropriate performance management in a democracy; 3) application of agency theory, or the notion that seeks to align citizens' objectives with agent incentives to achieve principled results; and 4) lessons that have been learned for improving future performance management.

Agency theory, which is rooted in economics and management, is difficult to implement in practice because of the complexity of values and goals among citizens and legislators. Heinrich gives the example of the Patient Protection and Affordable Care Act of 2010 (commonly called the Affordable Care Act [ACA] or Obamacare), which has several goals and tries to achieve potentially conflicting objectives such as affordable health care for all Americans, increased quality and efficiency of providing health care, and improved access to innovative medical therapies. But once the law has been fully implemented, it may have unintended consequences that distort its performance. She gives another example, from Michigan's Wayne County (i.e., metro Detroit), of children's service agencies that use performance-based contracts: children in this system were less likely to be reunited with their families and more likely to enter foster homes. The end result was that children and families received fewer in-agency health services. Performance-based contract agencies may also influence the way workers deliver services:

rather than drawing motivation from an ethos of public service, workers may find that their self-interest in such cases does not square with the priorities of the services they are delivering. Conversely, employees are more likely to take principled actions if they feel their agency and employment goals are aligned with the best interests of the public.

In another example of the relation of performance management to good governance in the United States, Heinrich asserts that poor-quality public education can jeopardize economic progress, even in a developed nation. Her case study of performance management in education, which starts with the 1983 K–12 report titled "A Nation at Risk" and continues to the present, shows that dropout rates remain high and achievement has not kept pace with other nations. Neither the nearly $600 billion spent annually on K–12 nor three decades of program reform have kept the United States from lagging further behind, she notes.

The author questions how spending, research, and reform could fail to improve education. She notes there are many factors contributing to this, one of which is that there are too many cooks in the kitchen, including the federal government, the statehouse, the local district, the individual, and the school itself, and of course parents or guardians. National monitoring of education through testing and standards has been controversial. The No Child Left Behind Act (NCLB), implemented by Congress in 2001, defines school success based on snapshots of student proficiency through standardized tests. Many have called this a factory-model approach, traced its roots to early twentieth-century manufacturing policies, and criticized its lack of emphasis on overall growth in student achievement. In fact, some argue that implementing such rigid definitions of accountability has backfired, in that it has led to a narrow emphasis on test preparation at the expense of deeper learning. Withdrawal and lower graduation rates leave behind some of the neediest students the law was designed to help. More-value-added models have since been proposed to account for factors outside the control of teachers and schools. Heinrich relates the experiments of others who sought to improve performance management through the use of multiple measures. These measures consist of diagnostic performance tools in which resources and rewards follow improved incremental outcomes. One such tool would be to reward measured outcomes determined by clearly defined learning goals tailored to the students' current performance and future employment needs.

In summary, there is no magic bullet. Neither more monetary investment nor strict adherence to testing performance has cured the ailments of the school systems in the United States. Heinrich notes the complexities of achieving a good performance outcome even in a wealthy nation, and she cautions that better guidance through governing systems can only be attained through confronting these complexities, with the goals of achieving desired learning outcomes and teaching effectiveness.

In Chapter 3, "Political Parties, Democracy, and 'Good Governance,'" by John Ishiyama, University Distinguished Research Professor of Political Science at the University of North Texas, Ishiyama offers an analysis of the influence of political parties on democratization in developing countries. He begins by acknowledging the historically negative public sentiments directed toward the very existence of political parties. He points out that none other than George Washington, the nation's first president, considered political parties to be factions motivated by self-promotion at the expense of the public good. However, most scholars have described political parties in a representative democracy as a necessary feature of that system, since parties offer political choices. On the other hand, a one-party state, while it cannot be a democracy, may still have good governance in specific areas. China, for example, succeeded in dramatically reducing poverty in the relatively short time span of about 30 years, or since reforms began in 1978. Yet China's one-party rule, and hence its lack of political competition, has made it difficult to solve problems in other areas, such as environmental maintenance, pollution control, and concern for human rights.

In Ishiyama's view, political parties are necessary to perform vital functions in the practice of democracy, such as interest articulation, political communication, candidate nomination, and stimulation of political participation. Encouraging these factors increases the potential for sustainable and accountable governments, including checks and balances. However, political parties can be so divisive that good governance is compromised; in developing countries this may even lead to violence. The shutdown of the U.S. federal government in 2013 by Republicans in the House of Representatives in defiance of the Obama administration is one example of political gridlock and extremism.

One-party dominance can cause an increase in corruption, since the dominant party attempts to maintain power by distributing patronage and using manipulation. Ishiyama holds that one can measure quality of governance, including levels of effectiveness and corruption. "Effectiveness" refers to the quality of public service and policy formation, implementation, credibility, and legitimacy of governments, used to promote inclusive polices. "Corruption" reflects the extent to which political power is used for private gain. It comprises both petty and grand corruption, as well as overall "capture" of the state by private interests. Both "effectiveness" and "corruption" utilize a scale ranging from −2.5 to +2.5. The World Bank makes the data available for parties in countries around the world, thus providing comparative data on levels of corruption. Using the same scale, political stability is also assessed. "Stability" is determined by the perception of the likelihood that a government will be overthrown through violent or unconstitutional means.

A recent case of a political uprising occurred during the Arab Spring of 2011, with the removal of President Hosni Mubarak of Egypt after 30 years of rule and the subsequent election of the Islamic Brotherhood party, which put Mohamed Morsi in power as president. This was not a stable environment, as demonstrated by Morsi's subsequent ousting by opposition leaders and the military because Egyptians perceived his regime as being exclusive of other groups. Many Egyptians were upset by his party's undermining of the role of women in Egyptian society as well as the injection of religion into politics. Egyptians may have been afraid that Morsi would create a religious autocracy analogous to the Iranian religious autocracy that emerged in 1979 when a popular uprising removed the monarchial form of government headed by Shah Mohammad Reza Pahlavi.

Ishiyama discusses the use of an empirical study that takes into account gross domestic product (GDP) per capita and ethnolinguistic fractionalization (a measure of ethnic diversity). He employs several measures—party fractionalization, number of parties, party volatility, control variables such as GDP, and other aspects—to attempt to quantify an average for how well corruption is under control, especially as it relates to political-party attributes.

The author stresses the importance of future research that explores what party characteristics can be determined to promote better understanding of governance. He also cites the need for better use of panel data, as well as improved model specification, to create more effective research assessments.

While the research into how to measure the effects of political parties continues, it remains clear that those parties created along the lines of ethnic and/or religious divisions cannot promote democratic good governance. By failing to be inclusive, they highlight divisions, exacerbate ethnic and religious tensions, and risk continued political instability. A mature, liberal, pluralistic representative democracy that respects individual human rights has the best chance of managing ethnic and religious diversity, compared to an autocratic regime. Social science studies of the relationship between governance and ethnic diversity show that multiparty democracies outperform autocratic regimes in the long run, especially in promoting citizens' rights, human rights, and the rights of minority groups.

Chapter 4, "Good Governance in Transition Economies: A Comparative Analysis," comes from Susan J. Linz, professor of economics at Michigan State University. Her contribution looks at metrics that draw a connection between governance and economic growth in the transition economies that emerged from the collapse of the Soviet Union in 1991. She discusses issues relating to the process of transition and to the measures of governance. Linz compares central and eastern European transition economies from the perspectives of both experts and business firms. She views governance as the traditions and institutions by which authority is exercised at the local, regional, national, and international levels. As such, she says, governance possesses political, economic, and social dimensions.

According to Linz, a state with good governance is participatory, consensus-oriented, accountable, transparent, responsive, politically stable, effective, efficient, inclusive, and equitable. It also follows the rule of law, controls corruption, enforces regulatory quality, and offers its citizens not only a choice but a voice. Linz identifies several measures of governance beyond the six indicators of the World Bank, such as Freedom House's country ratings of political rights and civil liberties, the Corruption Perceptions Index (CPI) produced by Transparency International, and the indicators of the Business Environment and Enterprise Performance Survey (BEEPS).

Linz considers these measures in comparing several factors that have affected variation across former Soviet Union (FSU) and central and eastern European (CEE) transition economies following the collapse of the former Soviet state in 1991.

These variations include culture, kinship, path dependency, financial and legal institutions, regulatory differences, and the role of foreign direct investment (FDI) on governance in each transition state. The FSU countries studied comprised Armenia, Azerbaijan, Belarus, Estonia, Georgia, Kazakhstan, Kyrgyzstan, Latvia, Lithuania, Moldova, Russia, Tajikistan, Turkmenistan, Ukraine, and Uzbekistan (15 states). Among the CEE nations discussed were Albania, Bosnia-Herzegovina, Bulgaria, Croatia, the Czech Republic, Hungary, Kosovo, Macedonia, Montenegro, Poland, Romania, Serbia, Slovakia, and Slovenia (14 states), for a total of 29 states. For those states, governance indicators such as CPI and the Freedom House Index (FHI) were used to assess political stability, accountability, and rule of law. From a business firm's perspective, she describes the influence of both macro- and microlevel policies on corruption, state capture and intervention, bribery, and kickbacks. She further discusses the effects of what are called "time taxes," a term that refers to time costs spent on bureaucracy—for instance, the amount of time that management personnel spend dealing with regulations, or, say, the average number of days it takes to complete business services such as import licenses, electrical and water connections, operating licenses, or construction permits.

Linz's general conclusions are that these transition states, with some variation, are plagued by persistent bad governance and corruption at levels from business firms to local and national governments. These indicators of bad governance were higher for FSU countries than for CEE countries. However, the perception of how many firms are tainted by corruption is higher in CEE than in FSU countries, even though transaction costs or time taxes are lower in CEE countries compared to FSU countries.

Chapter 5, "Governance Challenges in Education and Health Care in Developing Countries," comes from Seema Jayachandran, associate professor of economics and director of the Center for the Study of Development Economics at Northwestern University. Jayachandran's focus concerns the impact of governance on human capital in developing countries, with an emphasis on education and health issues. She argues that good governance is more critical in developing states than in mature democracies like the United States. For example, in Uganda, it is estimated that ruling politicians steal 20 percent of the money intended for education and health, which has a corresponding detrimental effect on the population. Teachers are compelled because of their low salaries to extract bribes and other services in kind from students and parents. In Bangalore, India, it is estimated that approximately 51 percent of community members have paid bribes, with some bribes for health services amounting to as much as 89 percent of the nominal service costs for hospitals and doctors. In addition, staff absenteeism in clinics and other health facilities runs as high as 56 percent. Worse, she notes, about 82 percent of health care workers do not have the appropriate documented training in the areas in which they serve.

The education sector makes up another area that does not offer much hope for success in developing nations with poor governance. In these nations, low-quality schools and universities abound. In some cases, teachers may be present for teaching duties only about 45 percent of the time. Eighteen percent of teachers are absent from class simply because of a lack of monitoring and supervision. Perversely, the low wages they are paid can provide teachers with an incentive to take on tutoring jobs while neglecting their regular teaching duties. A combination of lack of effective management and low teacher salaries prevents students in these areas from receiving the education the state claims to provide. In short, the educational problems of poorly governed countries cannot be alleviated without addressing the limited resources of local communities, insufficient school infrastructure, and the large, ill-equipped classes that result.

Jayachandran concludes by offering general recommendations for how to improve both health care and education. She proposes the following three remedies: 1) link pay and bonuses to real performance; 2) use digital technology such as cameras to monitor teaching and to supervise staff, including using cell phones and radio to improve monitoring and supervision; 3) empower local citizens, especially women, who are culturally more connected to children. Countries like Uganda and Kenya can use positive incentives such as hiring teachers through contracts that provide rewards and bonuses for positively monitored performance.

Chapter 6 is titled "Governance Problems and Priorities for Local Climate Adaptation and Poverty Alleviation"; its author, Stephen C. Smith, is a professor of economics and international affairs and directs the Research Program in Poverty, Development, and Globalization at George Washington University. Smith's concern is the interaction between poverty, the environment, and climate change.

Smith maintains that while there have been encouraging signs of reduction in poverty globally, much work remains to be done. Although improvements have been made, poverty traps persist, making it impossible to eliminate absolute and chronic poverty. He argues that climate change has the potential to exacerbate some causes of poverty cycles and that the negative consequences of climate change are carried disproportionately by the poorest two billion people on the global income ladder. As natural resources such as land, forests, and access to water become more scarce, the poor use more resources in an effort to survive. In doing so they often increase degradation of the land, resources, and soil, and they contribute to deforestation and water depletion. However, it is possible to instill planned and autonomous adaptation in local communities to alleviate natural resource depletion. Smith asserts that good governance can assist communities in climate adaptation and minimize the risk of environmental decline as climate change continues to alter weather cycles. Climate change is driven by both human and natural factors, and the human factors stem in large part from policies of unsustainable development rooted in a lack of good governance. Moreover, high-quality governance may prevent some climate-driven conflict that arises in impoverished areas.

On a positive note, Smith does point to some recent progress being made on poverty reduction. For example, since 1980, the fraction of the population earning below $1 a day (adjusted to $1.25 a day for inflation) has fallen from about 40 percent to just above 20 percent worldwide, and the World Bank reports that the goal of halving overall poverty by 2015 is being met in some countries of Asia. Even in Africa, 6 of the 10 fastest-growing economies have experienced impressive improvement in most health and education indicators, even though quality remains a concern.

In addition, there has been progress in the spread of democracy and transparency globally, even though all of the eight Millennium Development Goals (MDGs) outlined by the United Nations may not have been achieved. Unfortunately, climate change may jeopardize some of this progress. Challenges remain, as there is a growing concentration of poverty in fragile and failing states. These fragile economies tend to occur in environments where threats to the natural resource–based livelihoods of the poor are most dire.

Smith quotes the former U.N. Secretary General Kofi Annan, who characterized extreme poverty as "a poverty that kills." While there has been much progress, Annan says, the scale of preventable loss of human life driven by human actions remains horrifying in some countries such as Afghanistan, Chad, the Congo, Guinea-Bissau, Mali, Niger, and Sierra Leone, where about one-fifth of all children die before age five from preventable causes.

Indeed, despite improvement in some measures of poverty, health outcomes in impoverished nations continue to lag. At present, life expectancy in sub-Saharan Africa is only 53 years. In South Asia, nearly 1 child in 12 dies before age five. In low-income countries, the under-five mortality rate is 118 per 1,000. In middle-income states, the rate is 51 per 1,000, while in high-income countries, the under-five mortality rate is only 7 per 1,000 (Todaro and Smith 2014). Every day, nearly 21,000 children in developing countries die from preventable causes— over seven million in 2013 alone. There are many other severe health deprivations. Women with nutritional deficiencies are more likely to deliver smaller babies at risk of poor growth and development. Malnutrition alone affects nearly two billion people. Many children face lifelong disabilities. In many poor countries, parasites are pervasive and a woman dies during childbirth nearly every minute. It has been estimated that nearly 3,000 children in Africa die from malaria each day. Smith poses the question of why it is so difficult for the poorest of the poor to make further progress.

He determines that poverty traps, exacerbated by poor governance, make it difficult to break the cycle of poverty and hunger. Poverty traps include malnutrition, poor health, inadequate housing, high fertility, illiteracy, low skills, and low capital. Smith proposes further research on multidimensional areas of good governance for reducing poverty and promoting environmental progress.

Chapter 7, the final chapter, titled "The Challenges of Good Governance and Leadership in Developing Countries: Cases from Africa and China," comes from my coeditor, Wei-Chiao Huang, and me, Sisay Asefa; both of us are professors of economics at Western Michigan University. We explore the following five topics: 1) understanding and measuring good governance for sustainable development; 2) governance, development, and multidimensional poverty index (MPI) relationships; 3) the role of governance in sustainable development and poverty reduction; 4) methods of addressing poverty traps; and 5) poor governance as the driver of conflict, poverty, and corruption traps. We also discuss how regional and global engagement can assist states in achieving goals through monetary policy, global investment, and foreign aid. By considering such policies, political and economic institutions can be encouraged to use good governance practices to fight the effects of endemic poverty.

We define sustainable development as a multidimensional process of socioeconomic and political transformation aimed at enhancing human progress in all its dimensions, including the freedom of political and economic choice. We propose that a program on good governance, peace, political education, and conflict transformation should be instituted across schools, colleges, and universities to teach citizenship, civil society, and responsible ethical conduct. Without good governance and its guiding principles, the well-being of a country's citizens is at risk.

In the book, *Why Nations Fail: The Origins of Power, Prosperity, and Poverty*, written by Massachusetts Institute of Technology economics professors Daron Acemoglu and James A. Robinson, the authors illustrate how exclusive political and economic institutions drive inequality and conflict, leading to the failure of nations. For instance, although the two Koreas contain populations, cultures, and environments that are homogenous in many attributes, the people of North Korea experience a very different governance outcome from those in South Korea.

The people of North Korea are among the poorest on earth, near starvation, while South Korea is among the richest and most dynamic states in Asia. On the one hand, South Korea forged a society that created positive incentives, rewarded effort and innovation, and allowed freedom for its citizens to participate in economic opportunities. At the same time, North Korea endured decades of famine under repressive rulers from one family assisted by institutional repression, with no end in sight (Acemoglu and Robinson 2011). Along with other such examples from history, the MIT authors' research yields explanations for collapses of the Roman Empire, Ottoman Empire, Soviet Union, and other historic empires. The book also offers insights as to why an African state like Botswana can succeed while its neighbor Zimbabwe is failing. For example, in the 1980s, a decade in which most African economies were failing, Botswana scored economic growth that surpassed Asian tiger economies such as Hong Kong and Taiwan, while other African states experienced negative growth.

Moving forward, policymakers can learn from historic and present-day examples both of nations with good governance and of those with failed and failing states. With better institutional planning, as well as more effective domestic and foreign relations, the implementation of good governance can be encouraged worldwide.

For instance, the book imparts suggestions for the United States and China on how to build sustainable, inclusive, more equitable and egalitarian political and economic institutions. This objective would also have strong policy implications for Ethiopia and other African states (Asefa 2013).

In this regard, Huang and I consider the case of China and reconcile a puzzling contradiction between China's impressive governance outcomes and its one-party authoritarian system, a mode of government that seems to violate the commonly perceived recipe for good governance, especially in the areas of voice, accountability, and the rule of law. But a closer examination of China's governance model reveals that China actually practices economic, political, and legal accountability (and, to that extent, rule of law).

In addition, China's *neodemocratic centralism* and collective decision-making process may have some advantage in enhancing efficiency and good governance—as a case in point, there is the Third Plenum's decision in 2013 to deepen reforms. However, it is important to consider that China has a long history of civilization and a relatively less diverse population ethnically and linguistically compared to African states, which comprise over a thousand languages and ethnic groups scattered among 54 states. Most of these states were formed by European colonial powers, primarily Britain and France. The exceptions are Ethiopia and Egypt, both of which, like China, have a long history of civilization (Asefa 2013).

Economic development does not have a secret formula, Huang and I posit: success in economic development requires only good and accountable governance of a country's citizens. Examples where good governance leads to better outcomes for citizens include countries in Europe, North America, East Asia, and a few in Africa. Nevertheless, many countries in Africa have failed to fully utilize their natural-resource and human potential. Most African states that suffer from poverty have made intended or unintended governance choices to continue long-ruling repressive regimes and to prevent honest dialogue and freedom of expression, including peaceful constitutional transition of power. They refuse to learn from positive lessons illustrated both from their own past and from comparative experiences of well-governed countries around the world. We conclude by expressing the hope that African political leaders and governments will make a different, positive choice toward building inclusive economic, political, and social institutions in the twenty-first century. This inclusive, democratic approach to good governance can take Africa and other regions, such as the Middle East and South Asia, out of poverty and conflict. Democratic good governance would positively affect all sectors of the economy and lead to progress for the twenty-first century.

CONCLUSION

In this volume, *The Political Economy of Good Governance*, the six chapters that follow this introduction capture several of the key dimensions of good governance, as well as what deleterious and negative consequences may arise in its absence. The authors draw analysis and solutions from diverse sectors such as economics, public administration, management, and political science, in order to treat some of the most pressing societal issues of our time. They connect the importance of education, health, climate change, and poverty to address the challenges of creating a world where more countries embrace good governance policies to benefit their peoples. We invite readers to further explore the authors' ideas in the following chapters.

References

Acemoglu, Daron, and James A. Robinson. 2011. *Why Nations Fail: The Origins of Power, Prosperity, and Poverty.* New York: Crown Business.

Asefa, Sisay. 2013. "The Challenges of Good Governance and Leadership for Sustainable Development of Ethiopia: What Can Ethiopians Do to Overcome the Challenges?" Paper presented at the conference "Development in Ethiopia: Changing Trends, Sustainability, and Challenges," held in Addis Ababa, Ethiopia, September 19–20.

Kaufmann, Daniel. 2010. "Governance Matters 2010: Worldwide Governance Indicators Highlight Governance Successes, Reversals, and Failures." Opinion piece, September 24. Washington, DC: Brookings Institution.

Todaro, Michael P., and Stephen C. Smith. 2014. *Economic Development.* 12th ed. Pearson Series in Economics. Upper Saddle River, NJ: Prentice-Hall.

2
The Role of Performance Management in Good Governance

Carolyn J. Heinrich
University of Texas at Austin

What the people want is less government and more governance.
—Harlan Cleveland.[1]

In the social sciences literature, the word "governance" has become ubiquitous. Avinash Dixit (2002) describes an explosion of the term "governance" in the economics literature based on his search of the EconLit database, which showed just five occurrences of the word in the 1970s, 112 references in the 1980s, 3,825 in the 1990s, and, in the five years from 2000–2005, 7,948 instances.

In broad terms, Lynn, Heinrich, and Hill (2001, p. 7) have described governance as "regimes of laws, rules, judicial decisions and administrative practices that constrain, prescribe and enable the provision of publicly supported goods and services." Ultimately, governance determines government performance. Correspondingly, the goal or role of performance management is to determine how public sector regimes, agencies, programs, and activities can be authorized, organized, and managed to perform at the highest levels in achieving public purposes and desired outcomes. Or, in the "reinventing government" conceptualization of it, performance management is one tool or means for bringing about more productive and efficient allocations of public sector resources (i.e., more efficient, results-oriented, and responsive governance).

In *The Dynamics of Performance Management*, Donald Moynihan (2008, pp. 4–5) describes the beginning of the twenty-first century as an "era of governance by performance management." He asks, "How important are performance management reforms to the actual management of government?" and answers his own question: "It is only a slight exaggeration to say that we are betting the future of governance on the use of performance information."

In fact, performance management may be one of the longest-enduring reform movements in public administration, with origins that go back to the nineteenth-century writings of Woodrow Wilson (1887). Wilson proposed a "scientific" and more "business-like" approach to public administration, which was later picked up and expanded in the scientific management movement of the early 1900s. Scientific management promoted the careful analysis of workers' tasks and work arrangements, with the objective of maximizing efficiency by planning work procedures according to a technical logic, setting standards, and exercising controls to ensure conformity with standards (Taylor 1911).

Paul Light's (1997) classic work *The Tides of Reform: Making Government Work, 1945–1995* compared the philosophies, movements, and other management strategies that come and go to tides which ebb and flow, overlapping as one comes in and another goes out—a conceptualization that aptly describes performance management since the late 1800s. Performance management has been coming in and going out of fashion, or ebbing and flowing, for more than a century, although some suggest it returned in tidal-wave proportions in the late twentieth century. Indeed, a mantra of the early 1990s, "reinventing government," proposed reforming government so that it would operate more like a business—focused on efficiency and getting results.

This intensified focus on "getting results" motivates a central question of this chapter: how can performance management contribute to good governance and improved government performance (as defined by public preferences for the means and ends of governance)? This chapter will address four key issues concerning the role of performance management in good governance:

1) Our history with performance management—the effort to improve the efficiency and effective functioning of government—is long, and its origins in economics and business are reflected in the design of our performance management systems today.

2) Even in fairly simple and amenable contexts, designing an appropriate performance management system is challenging; the complexities of the public sector and our multi-layered, representative government system greatly compound the challenges.

3) What is the result of applying a promising governance tool in a rather blunt form that skirts the complexities of the public sector?

4) If we are, in fact, betting the future of governance on performance management, what are the lessons that we have learned to date that can be used to improve its effectiveness?

THE ORIGINS OF PERFORMANCE MANAGEMENT

To understand how performance management is viewed and conducted today, it is helpful to look back at the origins of performance management. It is largely recognized, in the works of political scientists as well as economists, that the roots of performance management lie in agency theory, as first developed in economics and business management (Wood 2010). The typical early performance-measurement system debuted in a factory production setting and was based largely on scientific management principles—i.e., its work processes were guided by technical analysis, and it established production controls and standards to maximize efficiency. In the agency-theory framework, the owner hires managers and workers to generate profits (with the owner or manager acting as principal, and the workers as agents). A key objective of the principal is to then design a contract that aligns principal and agent incentives and achieves the production objectives of the principal. This is made challenging, however, by the fact that these relationships are frequently typified by conflicts in goals and values, as well as privately held information or information asymmetries.

It is here that a role for performance management enters in—both in monitoring worker actions, outputs, and outcomes and in developing an incentive scheme with rewards or sanctions that align principal and agent interests—in essence, a contractual relationship with performance expectations and credible provisions for enforcing them. However, even in a simple production system that assumes

- organizational goals and production tasks that are known to both sides,
- a linear relationship between efforts and outputs,

- verifiable employee efforts,
- the dominance of self-interest, and
- a relatively small number of variables for managers to control,

an enforceable contract is difficult to achieve. In fact, in economics and business management, it has long been acknowledged that the richer (more complex) "real world" circumstances hardly ever correspond to the strict conditions of a simple linear incentive scheme (Holmstrom and Milgrom 1987).

There are two main challenges presented by agency theory that complicate efforts to establish viable performance-based contracts (Holmstrom 1982). One is the well-known problem of adverse selection, where employees' true motivations or capabilities for producing a desired outcome are unknown to employers (i.e., there is hidden information). The second is moral hazard and unobservability, in which employees' efforts or actions are not observable or readily measured; this creates conditions that can lead to shirking or distorted results. Recent headlines reporting cheating scandals in K–12 schools—which are under pressure to meet performance targets on standardized tests set by the No Child Left Behind (NCLB) Act—have illuminated a textbook case of how these problems can undermine performance management efforts (Rich 2013).

Yet many contracts and performance management systems still incorporate basic linear (or "straight-line") incentive schemes, largely because of their perceived simplicity and the significant costs associated with establishing a more intricate contract or system of incentives for inducing work and responsible management. A straight-line approach typically defines a required (linear) rate of performance improvement from an initial score or target level, and it may also specify an ending value corresponding to a maximum performance level, such as NCLB's goal of 100 percent proficiency in mathematics for public school students by 2014 (see Figure 2.1). No Child Left Behind is also an example, however, of an important shortcoming of straight-line models for establishing performance expectations: they are seldom constructed using empirical data or other evidence that would generate realistic expectations for performance (Koretz and Hamilton 2006). In fact, the U.S. Department of Education has made it clear that it is aware that the performance management system under NCLB is not working.

Figure 2.1 Annual Expectations Set by the No Child Left Behind Act for Increased Performance among Students in Grades K–8 Tested in Math, 2002–2014 (% that must be met of students testing at the "proficient" level)

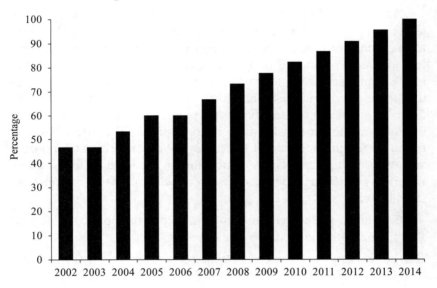

NOTE: Figure shows the expected percentage of students each year that should achieve a rating of "proficient" in testing for math under the legislation. The bar for 2002, the first year the law was in effect, shows the actual percentage of students who tested as proficient in math that year, and no improvement was required for the first year following that. But thereafter, increasing percentages of proficiency were set for each year, culminating in 2014, when 100 percent of kindergarteners through eighth graders were expected to be proficient in math. (The exception was 2006, when the expectations were not raised from 2005.)
SOURCE: Author's compilation.

As Secretary of Education Arne Duncan testified before the U.S. Senate Committee on Health, Education, Labor, and Pensions some two years ago, "The closer we have gotten to 2014, the more NCLB has changed from an instrument of reform into a barrier to reform. And, the kids who have lost the most from that change are . . . students with disabilities, low-income and minority students, and English learners" (U.S. Department of Education 2013, p. 1).

ADDED COMPLEXITIES OF PERFORMANCE MANAGEMENT IN THE PUBLIC SECTOR

As a matter of fact, from the start, the application of agency theory to the design of performance management systems in the public sector has been considerably more complex than many anticipated. First, just *who* is the principal in a given governance setting? Governance in the public sector is multilayered (or hierarchical) and dynamic. In the "logic of governance" model that Lynn, Heinrich, and Hill (2001) describe, actors can be identified as the principal in one relationship and the agent in another (as shown by the repetition of the lettered categories in the progression below). Or, one might characterize a relationship as having multiple principals, depending on the level of focus. Lynn, Heinrich, and Hill's model specifies a hierarchy of governance relationships between

(a) citizen preferences and interests expressed politically and (b) legislative choice,

(b) legislator preferences in enacted legislation and (c) formally authorized structures and processes in public agencies,

(c) structure of formal authority and (d) de facto organization and management of agencies and programs and their activities,

(d) organization and administration or management of agencies and (e) primary work of public agencies,

(e) primary work of public agencies generates output or results that are subject to (f) stakeholder/citizen assessments of public sector performance, and

(f) stakeholder/citizen assessments expressed politically and (g) public and legislative interests and preferences.

In addition, consensus or clarity on goals is often lacking among citizens, and sometimes in originating legislation as well. Consider, for, example, the Patient Protection and Affordable Care Act (ACA) of 2010. There are nine titles or goals of the ACA, but discord at both the federal and state levels since its passage reflects a lack of consensus about how we will implement the law and simultaneously achieve a number of its core goals, including

The Role of Performance Management in Good Governance   21

- affordable health care for all Americans,
- increased quality and efficiency of health care, and
- improved access to innovative medical therapies.

Furthermore, the implementation of the ACA is not only requiring cooperation across multiple levels of governance, but also the creation of new governing structures (e.g., health care insurance exchanges and other new forms of public-private partnerships for health care administration) that may add new layers of governance relationships.

The public sector is also distinctive in that its primary work or production technologies typically involve complex, nonmanual work, characterized by multitasking and multilevel interactions and public-private sector partnerships and coordination, such as in the delivery of publicly funded health care, education, and social services. Nonstandardized outputs make the accurate measurement of performance and the construction of performance benchmarks both more challenging and more costly. In addition, in designing performance management systems and incentives in new contexts, we often begin with an imperfect understanding of agents' means for influencing performance and their likely responses to incentives. The potential for unintended consequences as performance management and the use of performance-based contracts expand into unchartered public-sector territory is high (Koning and Heinrich 2013).

For example, market-based incentives were developed and employed in child welfare agencies in Wayne County, Michigan (the Detroit metropolitan area), with the objective of improving reunification rates and other permanency outcomes for children in the child welfare system. The performance incentive system was designed to provide a lower per-diem rate, with an initial lump sum payment to agencies for the provision of services and financial bonuses for the movement of foster children into permanent placements (and for sustaining them). McBeath and Meezan (2010) explain that it was expected that the performance bonuses would provide incentives to improve performance and would generate costs savings along a number of dimensions, including

- the rates at which reunification and adoption were secured,
- the time needed to achieve permanency in placements,

- rates of recidivism upon exit from agency care, and
- the number of youth in foster care.

In turn, the mechanisms by which managers might influence these child welfare outcomes included the services provided to children and families in foster care and in moving children into permanent placements (e.g., case management, supervised parent-child visits, and specialized services in the community), as well as the structural and technical aspects of service provision, such as agency staffing and caseloads per worker, worker training, service coordination, and supervision.

In their empirical analysis, McBeath and Meezan (2010) find that children served by Wayne County agencies under performance-based contracts were *less* likely to be reunified and were more likely to enter kinship foster homes, and that these children and their families received fewer in-agency therapeutic and nontherapeutic services and community services. In other words, the performance-based contracting system generated mostly unintended consequences. Although several explanations are plausible, it appears that incentives to reduce service costs and speed up the identification of potential permanency options for children dominated agency and worker responses, which led to reductions in important within-agency services. These reductions may have subsequently decreased performance on the desired outcomes.

Finally, the public sector is also distinct from the private sector in the extent to which political influences may be brought to bear at many different levels. Goals and priorities can change swiftly, and entire agencies or authority structures can be reorganized, as well as the foci of primary work.[2] This ensures that any performance management or incentive systems in public agencies will be dynamic. In addition, principals may also choose to change or replace performance measures over time, as agents (employees) learn how to (strategically) manipulate performance measures to increase measured performance in ways that do not necessarily improve outcomes (Heinrich and Marschke 2010). Widespread reports of teaching to the test, manipulating who takes standardized tests, and other means for inflating test scores in K–12 public education are just one example of gaming the system in public-sector performance management, and one that is motivating debate among education policymakers and spurring ongoing efforts to improve education performance measures and accountability systems.

APPLYING PERFORMANCE MANAGEMENT BLUNTLY IN THE PUBLIC SECTOR

Having considered the role of performance management in good governance from a more theoretical or abstract perspective, it is useful to work through some of the challenges in greater depth with a concrete policy application for an important, publicly provided service: K–12 public education. In 1983, an influential report, *A Nation at Risk: The Imperative for Educational Reform*, first warned that U.S. educational institutions were losing sight of their basic goals and high expectations and putting the economic well-being and security of the nation in jeopardy. The report set off alarm bells by pointing out that, when several educational measures were tallied among peer nations, the United States came in seventh.

Today, we are spending close to $600 billion annually on our public elementary and secondary school system, and the public is demanding greater accountability and results. Yet 20 countries now have higher graduation rates than the United States. Almost three decades of educational reform efforts appear to have left the country even further behind, and dropout rates have remained stubbornly high. Furthermore, public and private stakeholders in education are increasingly at odds over what types of interventions and incentives are needed to turn these trends around.

Indeed, public education today is characterized by elaborate but chaotic governing structures, widely varying views on appropriate means and ends for improving education and how trade-offs among goals should be managed, an increasingly complex technology with nonstandardized outputs (which we subject to standardized measures of outcomes), and political influences that interject their agendas at many levels. As Finn and Petrilli (2013) describe it, there are

> too many cooks in the education kitchen and nobody really in charge. We bow to the mantra of "local control" yet, in fact, nearly every major decision affecting the education of our children is shaped (and misshaped) by at least four separate levels of governance: Washington, the state capitol, the local district, and the individual school building itself. And that's without even considering intermediate units (such as the regional education-service centers

seen in Texas, New York, Ohio, and elsewhere), the courts (which exert enormous influence on our schools), or parents and guardians, and the degree to which all of their decisions influence the nature and quality of a child's schooling. (p. 21)

Drawing education governance into the "logic of governance" model outlined earlier, the complexities of multiple layers of education governance and the various actors (both principals and agents) at each level are apparent, as shown below:

(a) citizen preferences and interests expressed politically and (b) legislative choice (Elementary and Secondary Education Act [ESEA] and pending reauthorization of the 2002 ESEA that created No Child Left Behind);

(b) legislator preferences in enacted legislation and (c) formally authorized structures and processes in public agencies (the U.S. Department of Education and state and local educational agencies—SEAs and LEAs—with governing authority);

(c) structure of formal authority and (d) de facto organization and management of agencies and programs and their activities (a complex division of responsibilities between SEAs and LEAs, with the added challenge of constrained authority under NCLB);

(d) organization and administration or management of agencies and (e) the primary work of public agencies (the primary work of education is changing—it is no longer just about giving classroom lessons; services provided in schools and needs for them range widely and are compounded by unfunded mandates);

(e) the primary work of public agencies generates output or results that are subject to (f) stakeholder/citizen assessments of public sector performance (standardized achievement test scores are limited measures, especially when used to determine whether students have met proficiency standards under NCLB); and

(f) stakeholder/citizen assessments expressed politically and (g) public and legislative interests and preferences (pending reauthorization of the ESEA and waivers granted to a majority of states under NCLB).

The Role of Performance Management in Good Governance 25

Our current governing structures in K–12 education consist of deeply layered and overlapping levels of decision making, which open more potential avenues for influence by different groups at varying levels and with differing ideas and interests. At the same time, the lack of coherent management or clear lines of accountability is an ongoing, central problem in public education. As Hill (2013, p. 332) describes it, "Though every rule was made for a reason, no one carefully considered whether individual rules conflict with one another." Could the use of performance management potentially bring some clarity and coherence to K–12 education governance?

Despite the many complexities in this sector, we have, in fact, proceeded full speed ahead with regimes for performance management and accountability in education that include strong incentives and high-stakes consequences for many stakeholders. NCLB marked the beginning of an assertive federal role in directing state and local practices to meet student performance standards. Unlike the ESEA's first-phase focus on distributing resources to the targeted populations, the second phase sharpened the federal focus on student performance—what Wong (2013) has described as the emergence of "performance-based federalism." The federal government holds states, districts, and schools accountable for a comprehensive set of standards, including annual academic progress, teacher quality, and achievement gaps, and for developing assessments of student performance relative to those standards.

Still, NCLB defines educational success primarily based on standardized testing snapshots of students' performance, rather than on individual students' growth, and current funding and accountability systems presume "same-age cohorts of students proceeding in lockstep," says Wilson (2013, p. 96). As is consistent with the origins of performance management discussed above, Linda Darling-Hammond (2002, p. 6) of Stanford University describes how our test-based accountability system reflects a "factory-model approach" to education (as developed by early twentieth-century scientific managers such as Frederick Taylor and Franklin Bobbit), in which schools are organized "to process large batches of students in assembly-line fashion rather than to ensure that students are well-known by their teachers and treated as serious learners." She notes that urban high schools

> typically hold at least 2,000 to 3,000 students, who may see six or eight teachers each year for 45 minutes apiece. In cities such

as Los Angeles, teachers daily see 180 to 200 students, who cycle through the classroom to be stamped with a lesson as if they were on a conveyer belt. Teachers are asked to individualize curriculum for the needs of every learner when they have no way of coming to know their students well. Furthermore, the group of learners is much more diverse than at any other time in our history. Thus, the conditions for achieving high standards are lacking in many schools in the United States. (Darling-Hammond 2002, p. 6)

Recently, recognition of the limitations of proficiency measures under NCLB has propelled alternative approaches to measuring educational performance, particularly value-added measures. A basic value-added model compares the individual growth of a group of students (e.g., in a given classroom or school) to average growth of the population of interest (e.g., growth among all students in the state). Some value-added models are also constructed to account for factors outside the control of teachers or schools in estimating growth in student achievement over time. Although these are (arguably) better measures of performance than proficiency levels, should society be ratcheting up the stakes that it attaches to them, as we have recently seen in some large, urban school districts?

One of the most controversial recent developments in performance management in education has been the high-profile, public dissemination of value-added measures of teacher performance in large school districts, including those in Los Angeles and New York. Calculated by third parties (outside the district), the value-added measures associated with specific teachers were published in the *Los Angeles Times* (latimes.com 2011a) and by the New York City Department of Education (Santos 2012). The objective was to get the performance information directly to the citizen (parent) stakeholders, who could use this information and their political power to drive public-sector performance improvements.

However, in New York City, the margin of error in value-added measures was so wide that the average confidence interval around each rating spanned 35 percentiles in math and 53 percentiles in English, the city said. Some teachers were judged on as few as 10 students. In publishing the Los Angeles numbers, the *L.A. Times* acknowledged that value-added measures "do not capture everything about a teacher or school's performance." The *L.A. Times* also published comments from

The Role of Performance Management in Good Governance   27

teachers in response to the publication of their ratings. The following is an example of a typical teacher comment (or protest) of the value-added ratings:

> Please note that these ratings are based on inaccurate data. During my time at Westwood Charter Elementary, I have only taught Kindergarten (where students at that grade level do NOT take the California Standards Test). I have also never taught 3rd Grade in my teaching career. (latimes.com 2011b)

A study by Mathematica Policy Research (Schochet and Chiang 2010) found that the error rate for value-added scores (based on three years of data) was 25 percent. Therefore, a three-year model would rate one out of every four teachers incorrectly, and when only one year of data was analyzed, the error rate jumped to 35 percent.

It is widely known that tests are limited measures of student knowledge and learning, and that there is inevitably human and statistical error that enters into their administration. In addition, there are well-documented negative, unintended consequences to high-stakes testing—overly narrow and excessive test preparation, gaming the system, reduced effort and withdrawal on the part of students, and lower graduation rates—particularly for low-performing subgroups (National Research Council 2011).

Thus, a major concern with the direction we are currently taking with performance management in public education is that we appear to be treating test-based accountability like a magic bullet. Education performance assessments (via student testing) are just one tool for improving governance and accountability to the public for outcomes, and such testing will be a tool of limited use if we do not address the variety of governance challenges that plague our K–12 education system.

LESSONS FOR IMPROVING THE EFFECTIVENESS OF PERFORMANCE MANAGEMENT IN CONTRIBUTING TO GOOD GOVERNANCE

Primarily, this chapter highlights one policy area (education) where we have encountered challenges in designing performance management systems to improve governance and performance. The lessons that follow—regarding what we have learned about the role of performance management in contributing to good governance and improving government outcomes—could be applied to workforce investment, welfare-to-work programs, health care, child welfare systems, environmental protection, and other areas where we have ventured forth (and, at times, retraced our steps) in performance management. What are some of these common lessons?

First, the effective use of performance management demands not only clarity of goals but also their translation into empirical measures that accurately and adequately characterize our ends (or intended outcomes). Where we fail on either of these requisite components, the performance management system may risk doing more harm than good. In many cases, the data available simply are not up to the task. We have also learned that short-term, readily available performance measures often do not correlate with longer-term impacts (Heckman, Heinrich, and Smith 2002).

In light of these limitations, and recognizing that performance management in the public sector often grapples with multiple goals and complex production, we may be better off with multidimensional (or multiple) measures of performance to guide core agency work. A number of school districts and states are now developing these types of multipurpose, multiple-indicator performance management systems for K–12 education, including the New York City Department of Education, which is using multiple indicators to measure student progress, student performance, and the school environment (New York City Department of Education 2014). A potential trade-off, of course, is that a more intricate or complicated system and set of incentives would likely place a greater demand on public capacities for managing such a system.

A second lesson is that we often begin with imperfect measures of performance and then learn about how employees or stakeholders respond to them in implementation, including their weaknesses and how they might be gamed. We may less often get a performance measure or incentive system "right" on the first try (as occurred in the case of child welfare agencies in Michigan), but that does not imply that further efforts should be abandoned. For the many reasons highlighted in this chapter, public sector performance management systems will

The Role of Performance Management in Good Governance 29

necessarily be dynamic, and we should expect to replace performance measures or revise system incentives and other features over time.

In addition, caution should also be exercised in attaching high stakes (or serious consequences) to performance results, given the known challenges and imperfections of our performance measures (such as the teacher value-added measures that have recently been publicly disseminated). The awarding of performance bonuses, "naming and shaming" (as in the publication of teacher value-added ratings), termination of contracts, or retractions of program funding would best be backed or verified by multiple sources of quantitative and qualitative evidence before going forward. A counterargument frequently offered against eliminating high stakes altogether is that the performance management and incentive systems would lose their "teeth" and purpose. Evidence to date, however, suggests that individuals and organizations are highly responsive to performance standards, even when the rewards are minimal, such as peer recognition (Bevan and Hood 2006; Heinrich 2007).

Another important lesson that we are increasingly coming to understand is that performance management systems are likely to be more effective tools of governance if we focus more on their use for *diagnostic* purposes. That is, resources and rewards should follow their *effective use* in improving government and program outcomes, rather than for hitting performance targets. In the public education example, schools or teachers would be rewarded for using information on students' performance to help increase their learning, ideally measured in terms of their individual growth (i.e., not just based on test score levels or gains). This would likely be a more appropriate outcome to report publicly (for the sake of transparency), and, if measured sufficiently well, it would also be rewarding the right types of efforts to increase performance (i.e., not success in increasing test-taking skills but rather effective use of performance information to help students succeed academically).

One well-known example of effective use of performance management information to diagnose and address performance problems is the CompStat/CitiStat model, which has been widely used in policing, and in other public service sectors as well. Four basic principles underlie the model:

1) accurate, timely intelligence
2) rapid deployment

30 Heinrich

3) effective tactics

4) relentless follow-up and assessment

CompStat starts with collecting data, analyzing them, and presenting them in visual form, but the key to the apparent success of this system is how those data or statistics are subsequently used. When the data are presented in graphic form to organizational leaders and employees, questions are raised and solutions are discussed. But it is not a one-time exercise—employees in the agencies or departments continually return to the same indicators and reevaluate performance. They also reflect on the decisions that they make based on the data, with the goal of improving performance over time. To date, this CompStat approach appears to have worked effectively for the "meat and potatoes" of government—e.g., refuse collection, filling potholes, police and emergency response—but can it be expanded to more complex areas of government intervention, such as improving health care and education outcomes or reducing domestic violence?

And finally, why continue at all with performance management in the public sector, given the significant challenges, risks, costs, and the politics and messiness of governance? That might be best answered with another question: In its absence, how do we better guide our governing systems to perform at higher levels and more efficiently and effectively achieve public purposes and desired outcomes?

Notes

1. Harlan Cleveland was the founding dean of the University of Minnesota's Hubert H. Humphrey Institute of Public Affairs in 1972. He also served as President Lyndon Johnson's U.S. ambassador to NATO from 1965 to 1969 and, earlier, as U.S. assistant secretary of state for international organization affairs, from 1961 to 1965.
2. A well-known example of rapid agency restructuring occurred when President Ronald Reagan appointed Anne Gorsuch to head the Environmental Protection Agency (EPA) in 1981. Gorsuch came into her role with the view that the EPA was overregulating business and that the agency was too large and inefficient. As she sharply shifted the agency's mission, numerous career bureaucrats were reassigned, demoted, or pressured to resign, in an attempt to align employees with the agency's revised goals. However, EPA employees who identified with the former EPA goals, acting as "organizational stewards," ultimately thwarted Gorsuch's

efforts, which they did not perceive to be in the best interests of the public, and she departed from the agency after 22 months.

References

Bevan, Gwyn, and Christopher Hood. 2006. "What's Measured Is What Matters: Targets and Gaming in the English Public Health Care System." *Public Administration* 84(3): 517–538.

Darling-Hammond, Linda. 2002. "Standards, Assessments, and Educational Policy: In Pursuit of Genuine Accountability." The eighth annual William H. Angoff Memorial Lecture, presented at the Educational Testing Service, Princeton, NJ, October 30.

Dixit, Avinash. 2002. "Incentives and Organizations in the Public Sector: An Interpretative Review." *Journal of Human Resources* 37(4): 696–727.

Finn, Chester E. Jr., and Michael J. Petrilli. 2013. "The Failures of U.S. Education Governance Today." In *Education Governance for the Twenty-First Century: Overcoming the Structural Barriers to School Reform*, Paul Manna and Patrick McGuinn, eds. Washington, DC: Brookings Institution, in collaboration with the Thomas B. Fordham Institute and the Center for American Progress, pp. 21–35.

Heckman, James J., Carolyn J. Heinrich, and Jeffrey Smith. 2002. "The Performance of Performance Standards." *Journal of Human Resources* 37(4): 778–811.

Heinrich, Carolyn J. 2007. "False or Fitting Recognition? The Use of High Performance Bonuses in Motivating Organizational Achievements." *Journal of Policy Analysis and Management* 26(2): 281–304.

Heinrich, Carolyn J., and Gerald Marschke. 2010. "Incentives and Their Dynamics in Public Sector Performance Management Systems." *Journal of Policy Analysis and Management* 29(1): 183–208.

Hill, Paul T. 2013. "Picturing a Different Governance Structure for Public Education." In *Education Governance for the Twenty-First Century: Overcoming the Structural Barriers to School Reform*, Paul Manna and Patrick McGuinn, eds. Washington, DC: Brookings Institution, in collaboration with the Thomas B. Fordham Institute and the Center for American Progress, pp. 329–352.

Holmstrom, Bengt. 1982. "Moral Hazard in Teams." *Bell Journal of Economics* 13(2): 324–340.

Holmstrom, Bengt, and Paul Milgrom. 1987. "Aggregation and Linearity in the Provision of Intertemporal Incentives." *Econometrica* 55(2): 303–328.

Koning, Pierre, and Carolyn J. Heinrich. 2013. "Cream-Skimming, Parking, and Other Intended and Unintended Effects of High-Powered, Performance-Based Contracts." *Journal of Policy Analysis and Management* 32(3): 461–483.

Koretz, Daniel M., and Laura S. Hamilton. 2006. "Testing for Accountability in K–12." In *Educational Measurement*, Robert L. Brennan, ed. 4th ed. American Council on Education–Praeger Series on Higher Education. Westport, CT: Praeger, pp. 531–578.

latimes.com. 2011a. *Los Angeles Teacher Ratings*. Los Angeles: latimes.com. http://projects.latimes.com/value-added/ (accessed November 6, 2014).

———. 2011b. *Los Angeles Teacher Ratings: Vivian J. Lee*. Los Angeles: latimes.com. http://projects.latimes.com/value-added/teacher/vivian-j-lee/ (accessed October 21, 2014).

Light, Paul C. 1997. *The Tides of Reform: Making Government Work, 1945–1995*. New Haven, CT: Yale University Press.

Lynn, Laurence E. Jr., Carolyn J. Heinrich, and Carolyn J. Hill. 2001. *Improving Governance: A New Logic for Empirical Research*. Washington, DC: Georgetown University Press.

McBeath, Bowen, and William Meezan. 2010. "Governance in Motion: Service Provision and Child Welfare Outcomes in a Performance-Based, Managed Care Contracting Environment." *Journal of Public Administration Research and Theory* 20(1): i101–i123.

Moynihan, Donald P. 2008. *The Dynamics of Performance Management: Constructing Information and Reform*. Washington, DC: Georgetown University Press.

National Research Council. 2011. *Incentives and Test-Based Accountability in Education*. Washington, DC: National Academies Press.

New York City Department of Education. 2014. *Performance and Accountability*. New York: New York City Department of Education. http://schools .nyc.gov/Accountability/default.htm (accessed October 16, 2014).

Rich, Motoko. 2013. "Scandal in Atlanta Reignites Debate Over Tests' Role." *New York Times*, April 3, A:13. http://www.nytimes.com/2013/04/03/ education/atlanta-cheating-scandal-reignites-testing-debate.html?_r=0 (accessed September 17, 2014).

Santos, Fernanda. 2012. *City Teacher Data Reports Are Released*. New York: wnyc.org. http://www.wnyc.org/story/301783-teacher-data-reports-are -released/ (accessed November 6, 2014).

Schochet, Peter Z., and Hanley S. Chiang. 2010. *Error Rates in Measuring Teacher and School Performance Based on Student Test Score Gains*. NCEE Report No. 2010-4004. Washington, DC: U.S. Department of Education, National Center for Education Evaluation and Regional Assistance.

Taylor, Frederick Winslow. 1911. "Principles and Methods of Scientific Management." *Journal of Accountancy* 12(3): 181–188.

U.S. Department of Education. 2013. *No Child Left Behind: Early Lessons from State Flexibility Waivers*. Testimony of Secretary of Education Arne Duncan to the U.S. Senate Committee on Health, Education, Labor, and Pensions, February 7. 113th Cong., 1st sess. Washington, DC: U.S. Department of Education. http://www.ed.gov/news/speeches/no-child-left-behind -early-lessons-state-flexibility-waivers (accessed October 16, 2014).

Wilson, Steven F. 2013. "Governance Challenges to Innovators outside the System." In *Education Governance for the Twenty-First Century: Overcoming the Structural Barriers to School Reform*, Paul Manna and Patrick McGuinn, eds. Washington, DC: Brookings Institution, in collaboration with the Thomas B. Fordham Institute and the Center for American Progress, pp. 78–104.

Wilson, Woodrow. 1887. "The Study of Administration." *Political Science Quarterly* 2(2): 197–222.

Wong, Kenneth K. 2013. "Education Governance in Performance-Based Federalism." In *Education Governance for the Twenty-First Century: Overcoming the Structural Barriers to School Reform*, Paul Manna and Patrick McGuinn, eds. Washington, DC: Brookings Institution, in collaboration with the Thomas B. Fordham Institute and the Center for American Progress, pp. 156–177.

Wood, B. Dan. 2010. "Agency Theory and the Bureaucracy." In *The Oxford Handbook of American Bureaucracy*, Robert F. Durant, ed. New York: Oxford University Press, pp. 181–206.

3
Political Parties, Democracy, and "Good Governance"

John Ishiyama
University of North Texas

What is the relationship between political parties and "good governance"? The role that political parties have played is rather controversial in the literature. On the one hand, there are those who express very negative sentiments with regard to political parties. Indeed, popular sentiment is often negative about parties and the role they play in democracies. George Washington cautioned against parties as "factions" motivated by the "spirit of revenge" and by self promotion at the expense of the public good. Currently, political parties are almost universally viewed as the most corrupt of the political institutions in modern democracies. Parties can participate in corrupt practices in various ways—by "buying" votes, receiving illegal donations, and "selling" public decisions. The image of political parties as nests of corruption is often connected to the low trust in parties as political institutions and even to the low trust in democracy itself (Kopecký and Spirova 2011)

On the other hand, many scholars have argued that parties are indispensable to the operation of modern democracy. For instance, E. E. Schattschneider, in his work *Party Government*, advanced the thesis "that the political parties created democracy and that modern democracy is unthinkable save in terms of parties" (Schattschneider 1942, p. 1).[1] Although Schattschneider perhaps overstates the case, there is indeed a general consensus in the scholarly literature that parties are essential entities in the building and consolidation of competitive democracy. The notion of the indispensability of parties is rooted in the idea that they perform essential democratic functions, and that while these functions may not be the exclusive domain of political parties, they are thought to perform these functions better than any other type of organization (Dalton and Wattenberg 2000; Diamond and Gunther 2001; Diamond and Linz 1989; Webb, Farrell, and Holliday 2002; Webb and White 2007).

36   Ishiyama

These functions essentially involve six primary political-party functions. (That number is more or less consistent with other categorization schemes; see, for instance, Diamond and Gunther [2001] and Webb [2007].) These functions are listed in Table 3.1, below.

However, much of the concern with political parties in systems in transition is that they do not perform their ascribed functions very well. Parties in new democracies often lack coherent ideological programs and are unable to offer voters clear sets of choices. The programs that *are* offered are largely detached from citizens' concerns (Ishiyama and Shafqat 2000; Kitschelt and Smyth 2002), and corruption is seen as widespread in such parties (Basedau, Erdmann, and Mehler 2007; Holmes 2006; Kitschelt et al. 1999; Salih 2003). Parties in transitional systems are also seen as not being sufficiently rooted in society, resulting in high levels of electoral volatility as voters and politicians continually switch parties (Kuenzi and Lambright 2005; Mainwaring 1998; Mainwaring and Scully 1995; Shabad and Slomczynski 2004; Thames

Table 3.1 Six Primary Party Functions

Interest articulation	**Interest aggregation**
Receiving and accepting public demands and determining the process of placing issues on the political agenda	Aggregating demands into coherent programmatic packages in democratic contexts
Political communication	**Stimulating political participation**
Communicating political information, including structuring choices among competing groups along different issue dimensions	Promoting political participation, including party membership, but also partisanship among voters, and the political mobilization and electoral activities of parties
Recruiting/nomination	**Governance**
Establishing the electoral rules of the game, especially the procedures for determining who gets nominated	Forming and sustaining accountable and effective governments

SOURCE: Adapted from Gunther and Diamond (2003).

2007a,b; Zielinski, Slomczynski, and Shabad 2005). Such parties have also been unable to monopolize the channels of leadership recruitment; hence they fail to perform the primary function of recruiting leaders (Hale 2006; Mainwaring, Bejarano, and Leongómez 2006). In short, as Thomas Carothers (2006, p. 66) laments, political parties in countries in transition tend to be "top-down, leader-centric, organizationally thin, corrupt, patrimonial, and ideologically vague."

Furthermore, party systems in many new democratic systems are one of two things: 1) They are either fractionalized, unstable systems, where government is paralyzed by a highly fragmented composition, resulting in weak coalition governments ("feckless pluralism," as Carothers [2006], characterizes such systems), or 2) they emerge as corrupt, patronage-based systems with a single or dominant party (Kopecký and Sprirova 2011; Tanzi 1998).

Parties are also seen as not being sufficiently rooted in society, resulting in high levels of electoral volatility as voters and politicians continually switch parties. This leads to poor government effectiveness (Kuenzi and Lambright 2005; Mainwaring 1998; Mainwaring and Scully 1995; Shabad and Slomczynski 2004; Thames 2007a,b; Zielinski, Slomczynski, and Shabad 2005).

Thus it has been suggested in the literature that fractionalized and volatile systems are "bad" for democracy. This is because such systems are not really institutionalized. Institutionalized party systems are better able to promote stable democracy than less institutionalized systems, for a couple of reasons:

- First, more-institutionalized party systems enjoy considerable stability—generally, systems where the major parties appear and disappear, or move from major parties to minor parties and vice versa, are weakly institutionalized.

- Second, institutionalized systems have strong roots in society and bind parties and citizens together. In a less institutionalized system there is less regularity for voters in the articulation and aggregation of their interests, and hence parties are less able to perform the aggregation function which is vital for the functioning of democracy.

Three aspects of party systems' institutionalization are particularly important for the purposes of this chapter. The first is *party fragmenta-*

tion. Indeed, party fragmentation makes effective governance quite difficult (Duverger 1954). Many small parties in a system often create the conditions for weak coalition governments, which are particularly problematic during times of political or economic duress or crisis (which is often the case in the developing world). An often-cited example of the negative effects of party system fragmentation is the Weimar Republic in Germany in the 1920s, which had a highly fragmented (and ideologically polarized) party system.

Another aspect of party systems that is posited as having a negative effect on governance is *party system volatility*. Party system volatility refers to the extent to which voters are lacking a stable set of party competitors over time. Party systems that are characterized by many changes in terms of vote share or composition are volatile systems. It has been argued that volatile systems do not promote effective governance, for a variety of reasons. First, party system volatility reduces accountability. When partisan actors come and go, it does not provide the opportunity for voters to "throw the rascals out" in case they have made poor policy choices, because the rascals no longer occupy office (Mainwaring and Scully 1995). Furthermore, volatility significantly increases uncertainty, hampering the ability of politicians and voters to engage in strategically driven coordination and formulate coherent policies. Finally, it raises the stakes of the electoral game. This may have the consequence of weakening the democratic commitment of politicians, who may seek other ways to insure themselves against possible political loss at the next election—such as through corrupt actions or, even worse, vote-rigging and electoral violence.

A third pathology of party system development is the emergence of a *dominant party system*. One-party dominance has not necessarily been associated with ineffective governance in the literature, but it *has* been associated with the promotion of corruption. A major cause of corruption is political parties seeking to gain political resources by selling off access to office to the highest bidder (Katz and Mair 1995). One-party dominance leads to more corruption, as the dominant party keeps power by distribution of patronage and other manipulations (Tanzi 1998). Thus, one-party or dominant-party rule is seen as generally inimical to good governance, and it is especially associated with higher levels of corruption than more competitive systems.

Although the ills associated with party systems have often been suggested in the scholarly work, there has been remarkably little empirical literature that directly assesses the relationship between characteristics of the party system and levels of good governance. What *are* the effects of fragmentation, volatility, and one-party dominance on aspects of good governance?

The above literature suggests the following three hypotheses:

- Hypothesis 1: Party systems' fragmentation is negatively related to government effectiveness.

- Hypothesis 2: Party volatility is negatively related to government effectiveness.

- Hypothesis 3: One-party-dominant regimes are negatively related to control of corruption (i.e., positively related to corruption).

DESIGN AND METHODOLOGY

The following analysis is a first attempt at trying to assess the relationship between characteristics of party systems and good governance. The sample of countries used in this study includes 92 developing states that have had at least three "competitive" legislative elections during the period 1975–2006 and that are also classified as middle- to low-income countries by the World Bank. These countries were also not completely controlled by the governing party (and so would qualify as having a "party system," which suggests the existence of more than one party). In other words, countries entered the data set if the opposition controlled at least some seats in the legislature. (Thus, countries like North Korea are not included in the data set.) The time period covered begins with 1975, which coincides with what Samuel Huntington (1991) labeled the beginning of the "third wave" of democratization, and goes until 2006, the last year in which all data are available.

The dependent variables in this study include three of the World Bank's six Worldwide Governance Indicators, all measured from 2003 to 2010. The argument here is that characteristics of the party system from 1975 to 2006 should affect government performance in the more recent period from 2003 to 2010.

- The first dependent variable, *government effectiveness*, is conceptualized as comprising the quality of public services, the quality of the civil service and the degree of its independence from political pressures, the quality of policy formulation and implementation, and the credibility of the government's commitment to such policies. The values range from −2.5 to +2.5, with negative scores indicating less effective government and positive values indicating more effective government.

- The second dependent variable, *control of corruption*, is also scored from −2.5 to +2.5 and reflects perceptions of the extent to which public power is exercised for private gain, including both petty and grand forms of corruption, as well as "capture" of the state by elites and private interests. In this case, negative scores indicate less effective control of corruption, whereas positive scores indicate relatively higher levels of control of government corruption.

- The third dependent variable for this study, *political stability*, is likewise scored from −2.5 to +2.5, and is conceptualized as perceptions of the likelihood that the government will be destabilized or overthrown by unconstitutional or violent means, including politically motivated violence and terrorism. Positive scores on this measure indicate higher levels of political stability, and negative values mean lower levels of political stability.

Two of the primary independent variables, party systems fragmentation and party systems volatility, are measured by two commonly employed measures in the literature. The first, measuring the extent to which a party system is fragmented, is the "effective number of political parties" (ENP) measure. This index proposes the use of the Hirschman-Herfindahl concentration index to measure the fragmentation of a party system based on vote shares in the election or seat shares in the legislature. Using vote or seat shares in the computation of the Hirschman-Herfindahl index and taking the inverse gives us the ENP.[2] I include the average number of effective political parties for a given number of elections, ranging from a minimum of the first three to a maximum of the first five legislative elections after 1975. This, again, is to examine how earlier levels of party fragmentation affect later levels of good governance.

Second, to measure party systems' volatility, I use Pedersen's index of electoral volatility to calculate legislative volatility. Pedersen's index measures the net change in each party's seat share in the lower house of the legislature from election to election. It is calculated by summing the net changes in the percentage of seats won or lost by each of the parties from election to election and dividing by two (see Kuenzi and Lambright 2001; Mainwaring and Scully 1995; and Mozaffar, Scarritt, and Galaich 2003). This is written as

$$V = \Sigma \left| c_{i,t+1} - c_{i,t} \right| / \Sigma c_{i,t+1} + \Sigma c_{i,t},$$

where V is volatility, $c_{i,t}$ is the vote share of continuous party i at the first election (t), and $c_{i,t+1}$ is the vote share of continuous party i at the second election ($t + 1$).

The resulting score for each country is an average score across each of the legislative periods. Again, I use the first three to five elections after 1975 to examine how earlier levels of party systems' volatility affect later levels of effective governance, control of corruption, and political stability.

Finally, I examine the effects of a dominant party on measures of governance. For my purposes, I use the definition of a dominant party system taken from Van de Walle and Butler (1999), who define a dominant party as a party that wins at least 60 percent of the seats in the lower house of the legislature for the first three consecutive elections following the introduction of competitive elections.

In addition to the primary independent variables, I also include a number of control variables in the analysis that can affect levels of government effectiveness, control of corruption, and political stability. These include

- economic growth rates measured in terms of gross domestic product (GDP) per capita;
- average growth rate over the posttransition period;
- a measure of wealth (GDP per capita average over the post-transition period); and

42 Ishiyama

- the level of ethnolinguistic fragmentation (ELF), a commonly used measure of the extent of ethnic heterogeneity in a country.

In addition, I examine whether or not the country had experienced a civil war (given that such countries often face challenges in terms of good governance) and a measure of democracy as indicated by the average Polity2 score (a commonly used measure of the level of democracy) over the entirety of the posttransition period.

ANALYSIS AND RESULTS

Tables 3.2 through 3.4 provide the results of the analysis. Given the continuous nature of the dependent variable, I employ a simple ordinary least squares (OLS) procedure. Coefficient estimates are reported as well as collinearity diagnostic statistics and the variance inflation factor scores. Table 3.2 reports the results of regressing the dependent variable of the government effectiveness score against the list of independent variables.

As indicated in the table, party fragmentation does not affect government effectiveness, which is contrary to what was expected. However, both the emergence of a dominant party and party system volatility in earlier years led to less government effectiveness later. In part this may be due to the transformation of initially very volatile party systems into dominant party systems later (such as the case of the Russian Federation since the 1990s). Furthermore, this result would call into question the commonly held sentiment that political systems that exhibit a "firm hand" are more effective and efficient. The evidence clearly does not support this contention.

One interesting thing to note is that post–civil war states are significantly less effective (in terms of their effective governance scores) than other states in the sample. This is not a surprising result, given that civil wars often undermine state capacity, but it is noteworthy nonetheless.

Table 3.3 regresses the second dependent variable, average control of corruption, against the list of independent variables. The results demonstrate that none of the primary independent variables are related to the control of corruption. These results call into question the notion that dominant party systems tend to promote corruption more than other

Political Parties, Democracy, and "Good Governance" 43

Table 3.2 Coefficient Estimates and Collinearity Statistics. Dependent Variable: Average Governmental Effectiveness, 2003–2010

Variable	Coefficient	VIF
Average effective number of parties over first three elections after 1975	−0.025 (0.023)	1.159
Existence of dominant party over first three elections	−0.358** (0.154)	1.540
Party systems' volatility over first three elections	−0.009** (0.004)	1.077
Average GDP per capita growth rate over posttransition period	−0.461 (1.899)	1.401
Average GDP per capita over posttransition period	0.0005** (0.000)	1.392
Ethnolinguistic fragmentation index	−0.341 (0.301)	1.193
Post–civil war state	−0.280** (0.140)	1.139
Average polity score over posttransition period	0.016 (0.018)	1.358

$N = 92$
Adjusted R-squared $= 0.300$

NOTE: * significant at the 0.10 level; ** significant at the 0.05 level; *** significant at the 0.01 level. "VIF" = "variance inflation factor"; "GDP" = "gross domestic product." SOURCE: Author's calculations.

types of party systems. This is clearly not indicated by the results reported in Table 3.3.

Furthermore, as in Table 3.2, which shows that post–civil war states have less government effectiveness, so too in Table 3.3, post–civil war states are significantly less able to control corruption. Again, this is probably due to the weakened capacity of such states as a result of civil war.

Finally, Table 3.4 reports the results of regressing the dependent variable of political stability against the independent variables. Interestingly, none of the primary independent variables (average effective number of parties over first three elections after transition, existence of dominant party over first three elections, and party system volatility over first three elections) has any bearing at all on the level of political stability later.

44 Ishiyama

Table 3.3 Coefficient Estimates and Collinearity Statistics. Dependent Variable: Average Control of Corruption, 2003–2010

Variable	Coefficient	VIF
Average effective number of parties over first three elections after 1975	−0.013 (0.023)	1.159
Existence of dominant party over first three elections	−0.060 (0.172)	1.540
Party system's volatility over first three elections	−0.004 (0.004)	1.077
Average GDP per capita growth rate over transition period	0.045 (1.887)	1.401
Average GDP per capita over transition period	0.0003** (0.000)	1.392
Ethnolinguistic fragmentation index	−0.115 (0.299)	1.193
Post–civil war state	−0.328** (0.130)	1.139
Average polity score over posttransition period	0.011 (0.017)	1.358
$N = 92$		
Adjusted R-squared = 0.188		

NOTE: * significant at the 0.10 level; ** significant at the 0.05 level; *** significant at the 0.01 level. "VIF" = "variance inflation factor"; "GDP" = "gross domestic product." SOURCE: Author's calculations.

Again, as was the case with government effectiveness and corruption, post–civil war states are inherently less stable than other states. It should be noted that in all of the models, the variance inflation scores did not exceed 2, so there are no problems indicated with multicollinearity in the analysis.

Thus, in sum, the above findings do not suggest support for the initial supposition that party fragmentation would be negatively related to government effectiveness. Indeed, the number of parties (in cases where there are more than one) is unrelated to the extent to which governments are effective. However, party system volatility and the emergence of dominant party systems *are* negatively related to government effectiveness. Dominant parties are not particularly effective at government administration, and neither are highly volatile systems

Political Parties, Democracy, and "Good Governance" 45

Table 3.4 Coefficient Estimates and Collinearity Statistics. Dependent Variable: Average Political Stability Score, 2003–2010

Variable	Coefficient	VIF
Average effective number of parties over first three elections after transition	−0.012 (0.023)	1.159
Existence of dominant party over first three elections	−0.106 (0.160)	1.540
Party system's volatility over first three elections	−0.000 (0.004)	1.077
Average GDP per capita growth rate over transition period	1.539 (1.901)	1.401
Average GDP per capita over transition period	0.0005** (0.000)	1.392
Ethnolinguistic fragmentation index	−0.158 (0.301)	1.193
Post–civil war state	−0.938*** (0.137)	1.139
Average polity score over posttransition period	0.017 (0.017)	1.358

$N = 92$
Adjusted R-squared = 0.486

NOTE: * significant at the 0.10 level; ** significant at the 0.05 level; *** significant at the 0.01 level. "VIF" = "variance inflation factor"; "GDP" = "gross domestic product." SOURCE: Author's calculations.

where there is substantial turnover in the political actors involved in the game. However, these variables are not related to corruption and political stability, which might suggest, among other things, that the relationship between corruption and dominant parties is overstated.

CONCLUSION

This chapter has been essentially a suggestive piece, with the use of data to illustrate the relationship between party system characteristics and three aspects of good governance—namely, 1) effective governance,

2) control of corruption, and 3) political stability. Generally, the results indicate that either dominant party systems or volatile party systems are associated with lower levels of effective governance. However, neither of these party system characteristics are related to the control of corruption and political stability. This would suggest that if one conceives of "good governance" in terms of effective governance, then promoting a stable set of competitive political parties is probably a good way to go. This would add support for programs such as those sponsored by the U.S. Agency for International Development (USAID), which seeks to promote the development of stable party systems in many new democracies throughout the world.

On the other hand, party system characteristics have little to do with either the control of corruption or the promotion of political stability. This would counter some of the existing literature that suggests that dominant party systems are more corrupt, and that stable party systems would lead to political stability. As to the former, one can imagine a situation (as in the case of many competitive party systems in Western democracies in their earlier periods of development) where competitive politics bred corruption such as vote rigging, multiple voting, patronage, and the like. Certainly this has been part of the history of political parties in the United States, as well as in other Western countries, so it is no wonder that competitive party systems are just as likely to fail to control corruption as dominant party systems.

It is also not particularly surprising that volatility is unrelated to political stability (at least as conceived of in terms of the likelihood of violent overthrow). Indeed, in several cases in the West, most notably in post–World War II Italy, party system fragmentation and volatility led to governmental instability but did not threaten the political stability of the country. In part, this political stability was supported by a continuous group of political leaders. In other words, governments and parties may have come and gone in Italy, but the leadership elite remained intact, thus contributing to the continuance of political stability (in terms of absence of violence), albeit not government stability (in terms of the stability of coalition governments). Thus, at least in Italy, it is not particularly surprising that party system characteristics are unrelated to political stability as well.

These main findings of this chapter are, of course, somewhat tentative. There are a number of areas for improvement in the analysis.

Political Parties, Democracy, and "Good Governance" 47

For instance, perhaps the key variable affecting good governance is not the party system, but party organization characteristics. In other words, parties that are more internally democratic may be more effective than parties that are less internally democratic, for instance. Second, it would be preferable to use panel data rather than a simple set of cross-sectional data (albeit with a lagged set of independent variables). Third, there may be individual country effects that would need to be controlled for by a fixed-effects model. Finally, in terms of the political stability analysis, a future paper might examine the relationship between political party systems and state failure—perhaps by using some form of hazard analysis instead of the World Bank's measure equating stability with no violence. Whatever the case, understanding the relationship between party system characteristics and good governance will remain a fruitful topic for future research.

Notes

1. Although, historically, there has been debate over the definition of a political party in the scholarly literature, we use the classic definition of the political party as offered by Anthony Downs (1957, p. 25): a political party is "a team seeking to control the governing apparatus by gaining office in a duly constituted election." See also Epstein (1967), Janda (1980), and Sartori (1976). For an alternative and stricter definition of party, see LaPalombara and Weiner (1966). For the debate over the definition of parties, see Ishiyama and Breuning (1998).
2. $ENP = 1/\sum p_i^2$, where p_i denotes the ith party's fraction of the seats (or vote shares). See Laakso and Taagepera (1979) and Taagepera and Shugart (1989); see also variations of the fragmentation index: Dunleavy and Boucek (2003), Molinar (1991), and Rae (1967).

References

Basedau, Matthias, Gero Erdmann, and Andreas Mehler, eds. 2007. *Votes, Money, and Violence: Political Parties and Elections in Sub-Saharan Africa*. Uppsala, Sweden: Nordic Africa Institute.

Carothers, Thomas. 2006. *Confronting the Weakest Link: Aiding Political Parties in New Democracies*. Washington, DC: Carnegie Endowment for International Peace.

Dalton, Russell J., and Martin P. Wattenberg, eds. 2000. *Parties without Partisans: Political Change in Advanced Industrial Democracies*. Oxford: Oxford University Press.

Diamond, Larry, and Richard Gunther, eds. 2001. *Political Parties and Democracy*. A Journal of Democracy Book. Baltimore: Johns Hopkins University Press.

Diamond, Larry, and Juan J. Linz. 1989. "Introduction: Politics, Society, and Democracy in Latin America." In *Democracy in Developing Countries: Latin America*, Larry Diamond, Juan J. Linz, and Seymour Martin Lipset, eds. Vol. 4. Boulder, CO: Lynne Rienner; and London: Adamantine, pp. 1–58.

Downs, Anthony. 1957. *An Economic Theory of Democracy*. New York: Harper and Brothers.

Dunleavy, Patrick, and Françoise Boucek. 2003. "Constructing the Number of Parties." *Party Politics* 9(3): 291–315.

Duverger, Maurice. 1954. *Political Parties: Their Organization and Activity in the Modern State*. London: Methuen.

Epstein, Leon D. 1967. *Political Parties in Western Democracies*. New York: Frederick A. Praeger.

Gunther, Richard, and Larry Diamond. 2003. "Species of Political Parties: A New Typology." *Party Politics* 9(2):167–199.

Hale, Henry E. 2006. *Why Not Parties in Russia? Democracy, Federalism, and the State*. Cambridge: Cambridge University Press.

Holmes, Leslie. 2006. *Rotten States? Corruption, Post-Communism, and Neoliberalism*. Durham, NC: Duke University Press.

Huntington, Samuel P. 1991. "Democracy's Third Wave." *Journal of Democracy* 2(2): 12–34.

Ishiyama, John T., and Marijke Breuning. 1998. *Ethnopolitics in the New Europe*. Boulder, CO: Lynne Rienner.

Ishiyama, John T., and Sahar Shafqat. 2000. "Party Identity in Post-Communist Politics: The Cases of the Successor Parties in Hungary, Poland, and Russia." *Communist and Post Communist Studies* 33(4): 439–455.

Janda, Kenneth. 1980. *Political Parties: A Cross-National Survey*. New York: Free Press.

Katz, Richard S., and Peter Mair. 1995. "Changing Models of Party Organization and Party Democracy: The Emergence of the Cartel Party." *Party Politics* 1(1): 5–28.

Kitschelt, Herbert, Zdenka Mansfeldova, Radoslaw Markowski, and Gábor Tóka. 1999. *Post-Communist Party Systems: Competition, Representation, and Inter-Party Cooperation*. Cambridge: Cambridge University Press.

Kitschelt, Herbert, and Regina Smyth. 2002. "Programmatic Party Cohesion in Emerging Postcommunist Democracies: Russia in Comparative Perspective." *Comparative Political Studies* 35(10): 1228–1256.

Kopecký, Petr, and Maria Spirova. 2011. "'Jobs for the Boys'? Patterns of Party Patronage in Post-Communist Europe." *West European Politics* 34(5): 897–921.

Kuenzi, Michelle, and Gina Lambright. 2001."Party System Institutionalization in 30 African Countries." *Party Politics* 7(4): 437–468.

———. 2005. "Party Systems and Democratic Consolidation in Africa's Electoral Regimes." *Party Politics* 11(4): 423–446.

Laakso, Markku, and Rein Taagepera. 1979. "'Effective' Number of Parties: A Measure with Application to West Europe." *Comparative Political Studies* 12(1): 3–27.

LaPalombara, Joseph, and Myron Weiner, eds. 1966. *Political Parties and Political Development*. Princeton, NJ: Princeton University Press.

Mainwaring, Scott. 1998. "Party Systems in the Third Wave." *Journal of Democracy* 9(3): 67–81.

Mainwaring, Scott, Ana María Bejarano, and Eduardo Pizarro Leongómez. 2006. "The Crisis of Democratic Representation in the Andes: An Overview." In *The Crisis of Democratic Representation in the Andes*, Scott Mainwaring, Ana María Bejarano, and Eduardo Pizarro Leongómez, eds. Palo Alto, CA: Stanford University Press, pp. 1–44.

Mainwaring, Scott, and Timothy R. Scully, eds. 1995. *Building Democratic Institutions: Party Systems in Latin America*. Palo Alto, CA: Stanford University Press.

Molinar, Juan. 1991. "Counting the Number of Parties: An Alternative Index." *American Political Science Review* 85(4): 1383–1391.

Mozaffar, Shaheen, James R. Scarritt, and Glen Galaich. 2003. "Electoral Institutions, Ethnopolitical Cleavages, and Party Systems in Africa's Emerging Democracies." *American Political Science Review* 97(3): 379–390.

Rae, Douglas W. 1967. *The Political Consequences of Electoral Laws*. New Haven, CT: Yale University Press.

50 Ishiyama

Salih, M. A. Mohamed, ed. 2003. *African Political Parties: Evolution, Institutionalisation, and Governance*. London: Pluto Press.

Sartori, Giovanni. 1976. *Parties and Party Systems: A Framework for Analysis*. Vol. 1. Cambridge: Cambridge University Press.

Schattschneider, Elmer Eric. 1942. *Party Government*. New York: Farrar and Rinehart.

Shabad, Goldie, and Kazimierz M. Slomczynski. 2004. "Inter-Party Mobility among Parliamentary Candidates in Post-Communist East Central Europe." *Party Politics* 10(2): 151–176.

Taagepera, Rein, and Matthew Soberg Shugart. 1989. *Seats and Votes: The Effects and Determinants of Electoral Systems*. New Haven, CT: Yale University Press.

Tanzi, Vito. 1998. "Corruption around the World: Causes, Consequences, Scope, and Cures." *IMF Staff Papers* 45(4): 559–594.

Thames, Frank C. 2007a. "Searching for the Electoral Connection: Parliamentary Party Switching in the Ukrainian Rada, 1998–2002." *Legislative Studies Quarterly* 32(2): 223–256.

———. 2007b. "Discipline and Party Institutionalization in Post-Soviet Legislatures." *Party Politics* 13(4): 456–477.

Van de Walle, Nicolas, and Kimberly S. Butler. 1999. "Political Parties and Party Systems in Africa's Illiberal Democracies." *Cambridge Review of International Studies* 13(1): 14–28.

Webb, Paul. 2007. *Democracy and Political Parties*. Democracy Series. London: Hansard Society.

Webb, Paul, David Farrell, and Ian Holliday, eds. 2002. *Political Parties in Advanced Industrial Democracies*. Oxford: Oxford University Press.

Webb, Paul, and Stephen White, eds. 2007. *Party Politics in New Democracies*. Oxford: Oxford University Press.

Zielinski, Jakub, Kazimierz M. Slomczynski, and Goldie Shabad. 2005. "Electoral Control in New Democracies: The Perverse Incentives of Fluid Party Systems." *World Politics* 57(3): 365–395.

4

Good Governance in Transition Economies

A Comparative Analysis

Susan J. Linz
Michigan State University

Do transition economies—countries that transformed from socialism to capitalism in the 1990s—exhibit good governance? If so, is the incidence or degree of good governance the same across these former socialist economies? Answers to these questions illuminate conditions that affect a society's well-being; the quality of a country's governance system is an important determinant of sustainable economic and social development.[1] Indeed, some argue that the benefits of promoting good governance are so important that doing so has become both an objective and a condition of development assistance (Santiso 2001; Weiss 2000). Here, the objective is to document the nature and scope of good governance among transition economies, and to explore explanations for variation across these countries.

Why does it matter if formerly socialist economies exhibit good governance? In transition economies, the process of transforming from socialism (where planners' preferences for investing in heavy industry dominated) to capitalism (where consumer sovereignty rules) involved a significant restructuring of the economy. In many of these countries, not only was there a need to develop previously unavailable service sectors (financial, legal, retail, and repair, for example) but also to engage in extensive renovation of infrastructure and production facilities. Moreover, just as the transition process put a relatively large portion of the population at risk in terms of economic and social well-being, the dismantling of existing institutions limited the availability of domestic resources with which to provide an adequate social safety net. Consequently, transition economies required assistance, and assistance tends to require that certain conditions be met.[2]

Transition economies received international financial and technical assistance not only to facilitate the transformation process (decentralizing and liberalizing economic activities), but also to reduce adverse consequences to households and firms associated with the socioeconomic changes (macroeconomic stabilization). Many of the conditions upon which transition assistance was contingent were governance-related (Bräutigam 2000; Santiso 2001; Weiss 2000). For example, one of the foundations for establishing a market-oriented economy is allowing for widespread private-property ownership and, correspondingly, the protection of private-property rights. At the beginning of the transition process, when property rights were not protected and banking institutions and regulations were not fully developed, these countries were not forthcoming with the investment expenditures needed in the transition economies to renovate industry or develop new sectors.[3] Improved financial, economic, and social regulatory quality and rule of law were necessary to facilitate the type of institutional developments that promote investment. Indeed, Baniak, Cukrowski, and Herczyñski (2005); Bevan and Estrin (2004); Bevan, Estrin, and Meyer (2004); Pistor, Raiser, and Gelfer (2000); and others identify an extensive set of governance-related factors contributing to the receipt of foreign direct investment (FDI) among transition economies. International assistance became contingent upon successfully addressing these factors because they would improve the environment for investment (both domestic and FDI), which in turn would contribute to the successful completion of the transition process (Hellman, Jones, and Kaufmann 2002).

Promoting or establishing good governance in transition economies was also important because the ability to distribute assistance to individuals and organizations in need appears to depend upon the "quality" of a country's political, economic, and social institutions. In particular, the effectiveness and enforcement of rules that permit participation and call for accountability, and the absence of corruption in interactions within and between the government, civil society, and the private sector, not only promote good governance but also act to enhance the transformation to a market-oriented economy. Documenting the transition process from the governance perspective further illuminates linkages between governance and development.[4]

Finally, because transition economies encompass a relatively large number of countries and represent a significant and growing share of the international market, promoting good governance in these countries was linked to promoting global economic security and political stability. Without efforts to promote good governance in transition economies, the initial chaotic and economically devastating impact of the transformation process could have escalated into a more widespread and sustained barrier to global efforts to reduce poverty and promote a better quality of life. For these reasons, evaluating the level and variation in good governance among transition economies enhances understanding of the link between governance and development.

Good Governance as a Process

Introduced in a 1989 World Bank report as an objective (Santiso 2001), good governance is best conceived of as a process. Governance, generally, is the process not only of decision making, but also of decision implementation—a process that takes place at international, national, regional/local, and firm levels, involving both formal and informal agents and institutions. The governance process encompasses political, economic, and social dimensions, such as selecting, monitoring, and replacing individuals who hold positions of authority; developing and implementing policies to manage natural, physical, financial, and human resources; and promoting social cohesion, thus enabling vulnerable individuals and groups to experience inclusion and social protection (Kaufmann 2005).

Good governance, a normative concept, requires that a number of conditions are satisfied: that is, that the processes of decision making and implementation are transparent, accountable, participatory, responsive, consensus-oriented, equitable, effective, and follow the rule of law (Kaufmann, Kraay, and Zoido-Lobatón 1999). Good governance means that sufficient information is readily available to determine whether decisions are made and implemented following existing rules and regulations; that consequences can be imposed on those deciding or implementing policy; that all individuals have opportunities to express their opinions or cast their "vote"; that affected individuals' concerns or needs are specifically addressed; that different views of the best interest of the "community" over an extended time frame are explicitly considered; that no one individual or group has an inherent advantage in the process or outcome; that the adopted policies do not preclude or impede resources (physical, financial, human) from going to their highest-valued use; and that the legal system not only enforces the laws impartially, but also with an eye toward fully protecting human rights (United Nations 2013).

Changing Perception of Good Governance

While much of the governance literature focuses on the link between governance and development, there has clearly been a change in the perception of good governance since the late 1990s. Before the global financial crisis in 1998, the "Washington consensus" (Williamson 1990) dominated development thinking. Policymakers were persuaded that a limited role by the state was most influential in promoting economic growth. Indeed, a widespread belief that open trade, deregulation, privatization, and fiscal restraint enhanced development contributed to the result that these elements became conditions for international aid (Santiso 2001).

As events unfolded after 1998, however, the governance literature began to reflect a growing understanding that legal, economic, political, and social institutions that promote participation, strengthen accountability, regulate financial markets, enhance the rule of law, and provide social safety nets are important in the development process (Craig and Porter 2006). Rather than seeking to limit state intervention, as was called for by the "Washington consensus," there emerged in the literature a commitment to strengthening leadership at the national, local, and firm levels. As Santiso (2001) points out, the "targets" or conditions required of aid recipients rose from 10 in the 1980s to more than 25 in the 1990s; Kyrgyzstan faced nearly 100 governance-related conditions in 1999. It is worth noting that conditionality does not eliminate the situation where promises are made by an aid recipient to undertake changes and adopt policies consistent with good governance but then those promises are reneged on by the recipient.

To document the nature and scope of good governance in transition economies and explore explanations for variation across these countries, the next section, "Governance Measures," briefly reviews the issues involved in evaluating good governance and the governance measures most widely used. The third section, "Comparing Transition Economies," explains why transition economies typically are grouped into two categories. Section Four, "Good Governance in Transition Economies: Comparing FSU with CEE Countries," utilizes multiple governance measures to illustrate different dimensions of good governance in transition economies. Section Five, "Good Governance in Transition Economies: Firms' Perspective and Experience," focuses on how firms view good governance. The final section offers a summary and concluding remarks.

GOVERNANCE MEASURES

How is governance—the process of decision making and decision implementation in the social, political, and economic realms—measured? Kaufmann and Kraay (2007) provide a straightforward analysis of governance measurement issues. First, focusing on *what* is measured, they discuss the pros and cons of using inputs or outcomes to measure the quality of governance. Inputs include rules, regulations, institutions, and practices that have consequences for the processes of decision making and implementation. For example, rules-based governance measures such as the Polity IV Project or the two prepared by the World Bank—1) the Doing Business Project and 2) the Database on Political Institutions—consider such things as legislation that prohibits corruption, formal disclosure requirements for public officials, participatory elections, political competition, constraints on executive authority, rules for registering property or employing workers, and the like.

While it is relatively easy to count rules, regulations, agencies, and other inputs, governance measures based on input counts remain problematic. Little variation in rules-based measures occurs over time or across countries, which limits their explanatory power in empirical analyses of governance. Moreover, rules-based measures contain an inherent ambiguity: do a large number of rules or regulations or agencies signal good governance or simply underscore the likelihood of conflict among them? More importantly, the existence of a range of inputs does not guarantee their enforcement. Kaufmann and Kraay (2007) discuss issues associated not only with conflicting rules but also with the existence of an enforcement gap. They use this discussion as a way to introduce an alternative measure of governance that uses outcomes (e.g., the Global Integrity Index), focusing on the enforcement of rules and the lack of corruption. Kaufmann and Kraay (2007), Arndt and Oman (2006), and others note that, given that perceptions and arbitrary scales are used in compiling these outcome measures, they too need to be treated and utilized with caution.

In their analysis of governance measurement issues, Kaufmann and Kraay (2007) next address *how* governance might be measured. They discuss the role and relative merits of both perceptions (based on experts and survey responses) and objective data (counts of regulations, bribe payments, court cases, and so forth) in how governance measures are constructed. For example, while gathering information from experts (lawyers, nongovernmental organization (NGO) officers, government officials, executives, and commercial risk rating agencies) is a relatively low-cost endeavor, this method introduces potential biases that may undermine the quality or accuracy of the governance measure. That is, assessments necessarily reflect experts' views, and the data they elect to view informs their perceptions. Moreover, survey data collected from firms and individuals, the beneficiaries of good governance, may suffer from inaccurate responses (how does one elicit truthful answers about illegal activities?) or bias in either the responses themselves or the interpretation of those responses (how does one code a situation where a bribe is paid, but the benefit is sufficient relative to cost to result in the bribe not being perceived as an obstacle?). Yet, given that both formal and informal rules and institutions influence political, civil, economic, and financial transactions, perceptions provide more insight into the practice or process of good governance than simple counts of administrators, agencies, bribe payments, court cases, regulations, and the like.

This analysis considers a range of governance measures to more fully depict the nature and scope of good governance in transition economies.

The broadest, most comprehensive measure, and one where the requisite data are collected from former socialist economies, Worldwide Governance Indicators (WGI), is based exclusively on perceptions (Kaufmann, Kraay, and Mastruzzi 2010). The WGI measure encompasses six dimensions of governance: 1) control of corruption, 2) government effectiveness, 3) political stability, 4) regulatory quality, 5) rule of law, and 6) voice and accountability, using 30 indicators collected from 33 different organizations.[5] The data used to construct the six WGI composite measures reflect the perceptions of experts (from both the public and private sectors and from NGOs) and include survey data collected from thousands of individuals and hundreds of firms per country. For country comparison purposes, each of the six WGI composite measures is standardized to have a zero mean and unit standard deviation. Positive scores reflect good governance.

Freedom House, a private nonprofit organization established in the early 1940s by Eleanor Roosevelt and Wendell Willkie, conducts an annual survey of more than 190 countries to determine how freedom is experienced by people and firms.[6] The country ratings, based on questions targeting political rights (10 questions) and civil liberties (15 questions), are constructed by country specialists rather than from actual experiences of firms or individuals. The political and civil liberties composite measures are averaged to determine an overall country status of "free," "partly free," or "not free." Good governance is associated with "free" status.

The Corruption Perceptions Index (CPI), produced by Transparency International for the first time in 1995, ranks 176 countries (including former socialist economies) and territories by their perceived level of public-sector corruption, based on opinion surveys and expert assessments.[7] The composite index is constructed from information collected from at least three sources (for some countries, up to 14 sources) and aggregated in such a way as to make the CPI composite more reliable than the individual scores covered in the composite (Saisana and Saltelli 2012). The country mean value is derived from a standardization procedure that puts the composite index score between 10 (no corruption) and 0 (widespread corruption). Confidence intervals also are reported to underscore the uncertainty associated with the perceived corruption measures (Lambsdorff 2007). Good governance is associated with a high CPI.

The Heritage Foundation, in collaboration with the *Wall Street Journal*, annually provides an Index of Economic Freedom (IEF), which is constructed using 10 components related to private property rights protection, limited government intervention in economic affairs, ease of starting and closing a business, worker protection regulations, and free trade; each component is averaged into a single score.[8] This measure is used in governance studies because it includes dimensions that reflect the process of making, implementing, and enforcing decisions and policies that affect individuals and firms. The IEF uses data compiled by such organizations as the World Bank, the International Monetary Fund, and the Economist Intelligence Unit, generating a composite score for each country that ranges from 0 to 100, where 100 conveys maximum freedom. The country score and ranking are designed to reflect the degree of economic freedom exhibited in more than 175 countries (including former socialist economies).[9] Thus, good governance is associated with a high IEF score.

An alternative way to assess good governance is from the perspective of the beneficiaries, such as firms. The European Bank for Reconstruction and Development (EBRD), in collaboration with the World Bank, began in 1999 conducting a Business Environment and Enterprise Performance Survey (BEEPS), which involves, in the most recent round (2008–2009), some 11,800 firms in 29 countries.[10] The survey is designed to track changes in the business environment over time and get information from firms about the nature and scope of the state's influence over private-sector activities. In particular, the survey addresses a number of factors related to perceptions of the quality of the business environment, the incidence and magnitude of corruption, and problems associated with corruption in transition economies. BEEPS data allow for the assessment of governance quality from the firm's perspective.[11] For example, the microdata permit analysis of two basic types of corrupt transactions: in one type of transaction, state agents obtain unwarranted benefits from the private sector ("grabbing hand"); in the other type, private-sector agents obtain unwarranted benefits from the state ("state capture") (Frye and Shleifer 1997; Hellman et al. 2000; Shleifer and Vishny 1998).

COMPARING TRANSITION ECONOMIES

How do transition economies fare with regard to good governance? Since the primary objective here is to document the nature and scope of good governance in transition economies, it is useful to consider two

Good Governance in Transition Economies 59

groups of countries: 1) those that were part of the former Soviet Union (FSU)[12] and 2) those located in central and eastern Europe (CEE).[13] The distinction between FSU and CEE countries stems in part from the duration of the socialist experience and in part from prior experience with a market economy.

Except for the Baltic republics (Estonia, Latvia, and Lithuania), FSU countries had very little experience with market-oriented institutions before the transition began in the early 1990s. Most FSU countries had exhibited a tradition-oriented feudal-type economic structure before the socialist revolution introduced central planning as a way to organize production and distribution. Under Soviet socialism, neither markets nor scarcity prices were used to allocate resources, materials, labor, or goods. Private property, in the productive sense, was prohibited. Formally, for over seven decades, economic decision making was highly centralized. Transactions were governed by the state, with no regard for profit motive and little, if any, regard for efficiency. Informally, individuals and firms often acted in their own self-interest rather than the state's interest, and they traded in ways that mimicked market-oriented outcomes. However, unlike most transactions in market economies, informal transactions in FSU countries, particularly Russia, were rarely quid pro quo. Instead, the culture of kinship and reciprocity governed social, political, and economic transactions (Ledeneva 1998; Volkov 2000). This culture, combined with widespread shortages in the Soviet economy of basic household goods and material inputs to firms, created conditions where those who held a monopoly position (from bureaucrats to salespeople) routinely exploited that position (Shlapentokh 2013).

CEE countries, obliged after World War II to terminate their market-oriented institutions and adopt the Soviet centrally administered structure, experienced a shorter-duration and somewhat different variety of socialism than FSU countries. Poland, for example, retained private agriculture rather than impose Soviet-style collectivized agriculture. Hungary and Czechoslovakia continued to participate in international markets. In contrast to the highly centralized Soviet model, Yugoslavia introduced greater decision making by worker collectives. When the Berlin Wall fell in 1989, CEE countries reestablished their market-oriented institutions. Unlike FSU countries, from the very beginning of the transition process CEE countries were populated with individuals experienced not only in working within the legal and financial infrastructures that support a market economy, but also within a decentralized social and political environment.

Thus, the duration of the socialist experience and prior experience with market-oriented institutions provide a simple way to separate transition economies into two groups for good-governance comparison purposes.

GOOD GOVERNANCE IN TRANSITION ECONOMIES: COMPARING FSU WITH CEE COUNTRIES

How well do transition economies fare with regard to good governance? How much difference is there over the course of the transition process? Is there a significant difference between FSU and CEE countries in terms of good governance? To address these questions, this section considers multiple governance measures.

WGI Measures

The Worldwide Governance Indicators (WGI) encompass six categories of indicators that reflect different dimensions of good governance. Since each of the composite indicators of WGI is standardized to have a zero mean and unit standard deviation, a positive score reflects good governance, and a negative score reflects the opposite. As seen in Figure 4.1, which captures WGI scores for the six composite measures for 2011, CEE countries consistently score in the positive range and FSU countries consistently score in the negative range. The governance contrast between FSU and CEE countries is the greatest for *voice and accountability*,[14] with CEE countries scoring relatively high (second only to *regulatory quality*), and FSU countries scoring relatively poorly (worse than in every category except *control of corruption*). Both FSU and CEE countries perform relatively poorly on the *control of corruption* composite measure.[15]

Because good governance often is linked to anticorruption measures (Kaufmann 2005), and because corruption (bad governance) is well documented in transition economies (see Abed and Davoodi [2000]; Hamadi,

Good Governance in Transition Economies 61

Figure 4.1 Worldwide Governance Indicators in Transition Economies

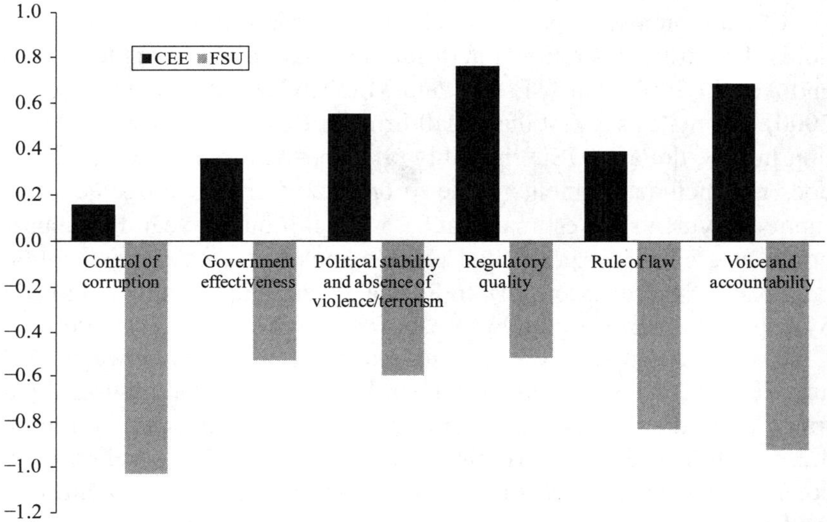

SOURCE: World Bank (2014). Data are for 2011; regional averages were weighted by population.

Rihab, and Lotfi [2009]; Hellman et al. [2000]; Shlapentokh [2013]; Steves and Rousso [2003]; and Tonoyan et al. [2010], for example), it makes sense to provide some discussion of this topic here. Perhaps most striking is the large literature related to corruption in former socialist economies: in April 2013, Google Scholar listed over 110,000 entries. In part, the literature is large because corruption involves a broad set of activities, varying by purpose[16] and the agents or agencies involved.[17] In part, the large corruption literature stems from ongoing efforts to measure and document corruption and estimate the costs it imposes.

Corruption is costly from an opportunity cost perspective because public resources are not going to their highest-valued use, but instead are being diverted for personal gain (Mauro 1995). Corruption contributes to lower tax revenues, which in turn reduce public services provided to the society as a whole. Social welfare is lower than it otherwise need be; wealth disparities grow. Corruption weakens formal institutions (legal, financial), which undermines the development process generally and the pace of economic transformation for these former socialist countries. In particular, corruption undermines competition, which is one of the pillars of a market-oriented economy.

Corruption also imposes direct financial costs on firms and households. For firms, operational and transactional costs are higher (Aidis and Adachi 2007; Aidis, Estrin, and Mickiewicz 2008; Johnson et al. 2000). Estimates suggest that small firms in Russia pay over $500 million in U.S. dollars (USD) monthly on bribes to officials, a figure that does not include payments made to organized crime; altogether, corruption payments are estimated at $10–$20 billion per year. For households, prices paid for goods and services include the cost of corruption (kickbacks, bribes, extortion). In Russia, corruption is estimated to add 5–15 percent to prices paid by consumers (Levin and Satarov 2000).

The general pattern of good-governance differences between FSU and CEE countries evident for the six WGI composite measures illustrated in Figure 4.1 also is evident, albeit on a smaller scale, in Figure 4.2, which focuses on the levels and trends of *control of corruption* by country.[18] CEE countries (shaded darker but not individually identified) tend to score higher as the transition process progresses, although, initially, half of these countries exhibit scores comparable to the majority of FSU countries (shaded lighter but not identified).[19]

One explanation for the relatively small differences in control of corruption involves the nature and scope of formal and informal institutions in FSU and CEE countries.

Tonoyan et al. (2010) explain how formal institutions contribute to corruption: too many (and conflicting) economic and financial regulations create obstacles, which provide opportunities to engage in rent-seeking behavior (corruption) as individuals and firms try to find ways around these barriers. Failure to enforce the multitude of formal rules further contributes to rent-seeking behavior.

Tradition, customs, and norms contribute to informal institutions that help to generate an environment in which corrupt behavior thrives. For example, in societies where kinship and reciprocity are important cultural features, informal institutions tend to be more prevalent. However, informal institutions themselves need not contribute to corruption. In some instances, informal institutions complement formal institutions by strengthening efforts to comply with anticorruption agencies and regulations (Tonoyan et al. 2010). Where informal institutions replace formal procedures, then corrupt behavior thrives. Dyker

Good Governance in Transition Economies 63

Figure 4.2 Control of Corruption in FSU and CEE Countries

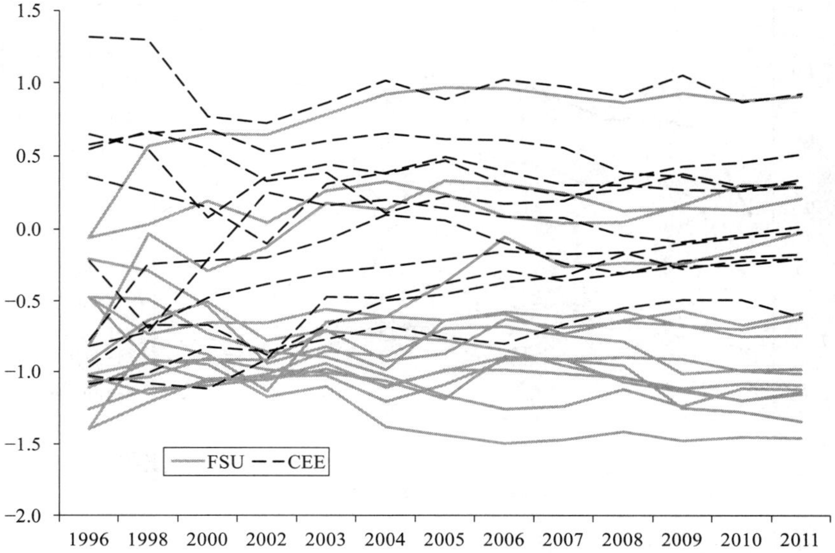

SOURCE: World Bank (2014).

(2012), Shlapentokh (2013), and others explain why the Soviet legacy of informal institutions is stronger in Russia and other FSU countries than in CEE countries. Moreover, the literature suggests that in societies where closed social networks predominate, and thus there is greater reliance on kinship or reciprocity, there will be a much greater likelihood that corrupt behavior will be sustained. This is particularly true where social norms are governed by the belief that good ends justify means (or that whatever works is correct), and widespread (illegal) behavior is consistent with this belief (Ledeneva 1998; Volkov 2000).

Figures 4.3 and 4.4 illustrate differences in *control of corruption* for individual FSU and CEE countries, respectively. As seen in Figure 4.3, for the majority of FSU countries, there is no real improvement in *control of corruption* over time; in some instances, performance worsens on this governance measure. Levin and Satarov (2000) and Tonoyan et al. (2010) make the "path dependency" case: societies that start with a high level of corruption will find it hard to reduce it.

Figure 4.3 Control of Corruption in FSU Countries

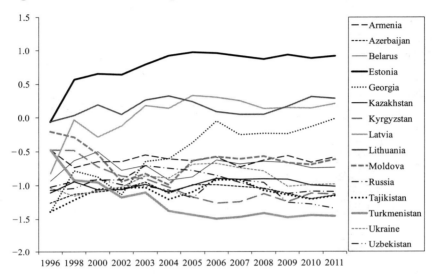

SOURCE: World Bank (2014).

Figure 4.4 Control of Corruption in CEE Countries

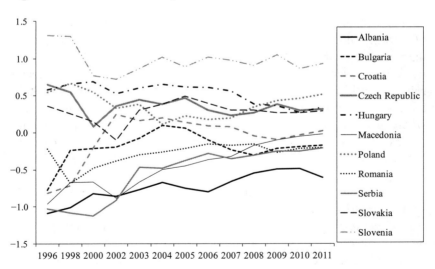

SOURCE: World Bank (2014).

Why do FSU countries have a high level of corruption? The Soviet legacy of a seller's market created conditions that obliged individuals and firms to circumvent official channels, which led to the widespread acceptance of the notion "the ends justify the means," which further fueled corrupt (illegal) behavior. Shlapentokh (2013) focuses on the influence of feudal tendencies and big money as the driving force for corruption in FSU countries, particularly Russia. He also describes the strata of "little bribers" who extort money: medical personnel, educators, inspectors, clerks, traffic officers, and the like. The fact that so many in Russia benefit from corruption contributes to widespread tolerance of corrupt behavior.[20]

In contrast, several CEE countries (Figure 4.4), likely influenced by European Union admission requirements, tended to improve corruption control as the transition progressed. Bardhan and Mookherjee (2000) develop a theoretical model to explain why some countries are more susceptible to "state capture"; the characteristics they include coincide more closely with cultural and other conditions in FSU countries than in CEE countries.

The ability to exhibit good governance is influenced by susceptibility to "state capture," which in turn has consequences for perceptions of *government effectiveness*.[21] While FSU countries perform relatively well on this measure in comparison to other WGI measures (see Figure 4.1), it appears to coincide with perceptions of firms and individuals that even though the "grabbing hand" of government is expensive, the benefits associated with informal payments are certain (Millar 1996; Shlapentokh 2013). As seen in Figure 4.5, with few exceptions, little change in perceptions of *government effectiveness* occurs among FSU countries over the course of the transition. Where perceptions improve (see Figure 4.6), it is mostly among FSU countries that have a positive score (exhibit relatively good governance on this dimension). Among CEE countries, two groups are evident: 1) those where government effectiveness is viewed relatively positively, and 2) those where the initial perceptions were negative, but over the course of the transition these perceptions improved (see Figure 4.7).

The relative performance of FSU and CEE countries on a related governance dimension, *regulatory quality*,[22] is illustrated in Figure 4.8. On this dimension, the majority of CEE countries (shaded darker) score relatively high, and consistently so. Among FSU countries (shaded

Figure 4.5 Government Effectiveness in FSU and CEE Countries

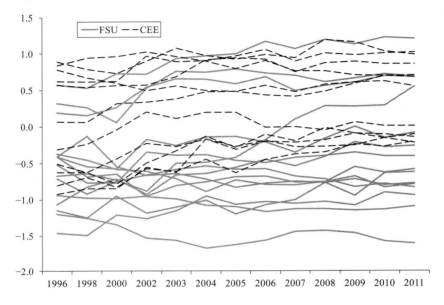

SOURCE: World Bank (2014).

Figure 4.6 Government Effectiveness in FSU Countries

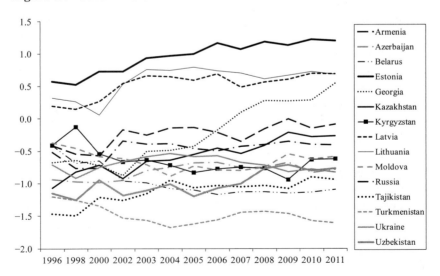

SOURCE: World Bank (2014).

Good Governance in Transition Economies 67

Figure 4.7 Government Effectiveness in CEE Countries

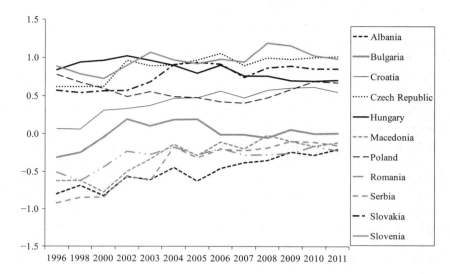

SOURCE: World Bank (2014).

Figure 4.8 Regulatory Quality in FSU and CEE Countries

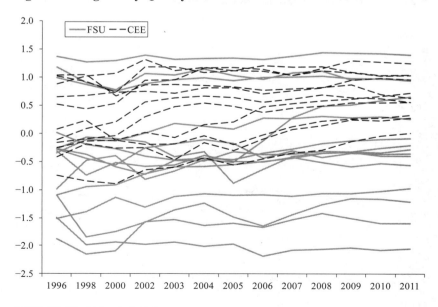

SOURCE: World Bank (2014).

lighter), there appears to be a similar consistency over time for *regulatory quality*, but the countries fall into three groups in terms of general score on this measure (see Figure 4.9). CEE countries tend to exhibit an upward trend over the course of the transition (Figure 4.10).

Figure 4.11 depicts *rule of law* for FSU and CEE countries. While there is some dispersion among CEE countries (darker) which contributes to their composite score being relatively low (see Figure 4.1), for all but three FSU countries (lighter), perceived rule of law is consistently in the negative range. As seen in Figure 4.12, for some FSU countries, the measure declines in value. In contrast, among CEE countries (Figure 4.13), there appears to be an improvement on this governance dimension over the course of the transition. Differences between the two groups of transition economies, and trends in each over time, may reflect differences in the formal legal systems in the countries: even if the same laws are on the books, they may not be enforced in the same way (Berkowitz, Pistor, and Richard 2003; Pistor, Raiser, and Gelfer 2000); judicial institutions may process different types of cases or with different priorities. For rule of law to prevail, judges, prosecutors, police, and court functionaries need to act honestly and autonomously

Figure 4.9 Regulatory Quality in FSU Countries

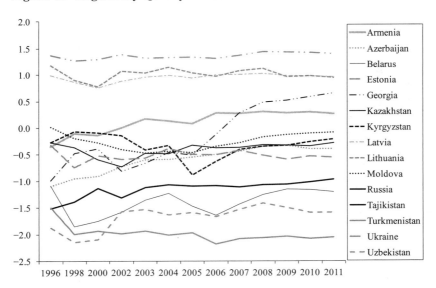

SOURCE: World Bank (2014).

Good Governance in Transition Economies 69

Figure 4.10 Regulatory Quality in CEE Countries

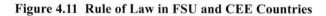

SOURCE: World Bank (2014).

Figure 4.11 Rule of Law in FSU and CEE Countries

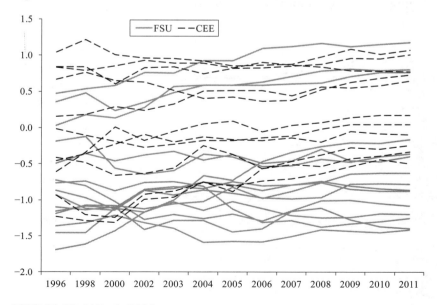

SOURCE: World Bank (2014).

70 Linz

Figure 4.12 Rule of Law in FSU Countries

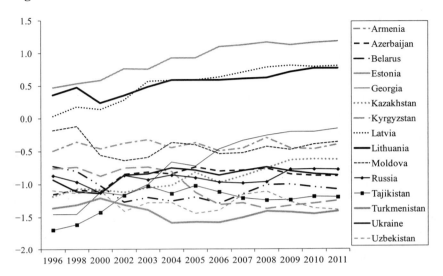

SOURCE: World Bank (2014).

Figure 4.13 Rule of Law in CEE Countries

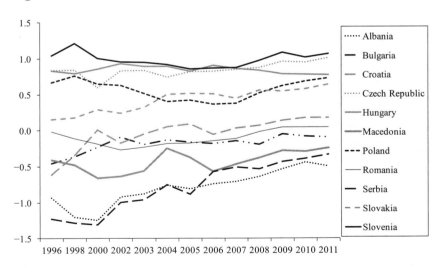

SOURCE: World Bank (2014).

with regard to the state and private-sector agents (EBRD 1999). Differences may also stem from country variation in commitment to supporting the type of individual rights and fiduciary responsibilities that facilitate emergence of a competitive market environment.

Differences over time between FSU and CEE countries on *voice and accountability* are depicted in Figure 4.14. A clear pattern of separation is evident. Even among FSU countries, a clear pattern of separation is also evident (see Figure 4.15), with the Baltic republics scoring consistently higher. For many other FSU countries, the score on this governance measure tends to decline. A steady improvement over time among CEE countries is seen in Figure 4.16.

Differences between FSU and CEE countries in the final component of the WGI governance measures are illustrated in Figure 4.17: *political stability*.[23] In comparison to the other five governance dimensions, there is more variability in *political stability* among CEE and FSU countries over the course of the transition. As seen in Figure 4.18, there is more dispersion among FSU countries on this measure as well. Not surpris-

Figure 4.14 Voice and Accountability in FSU and CEE Countries

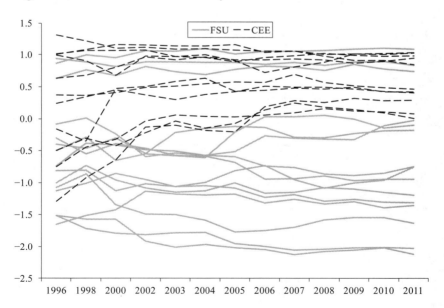

SOURCE: World Bank (2014).

72 Linz

Figure 4.15 Voice and Accountability in FSU Countries

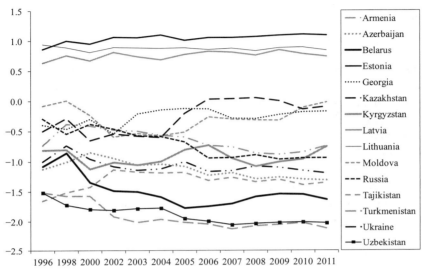

SOURCE: World Bank (2014).

Figure 4.16 Voice and Accountability in CEE Countries

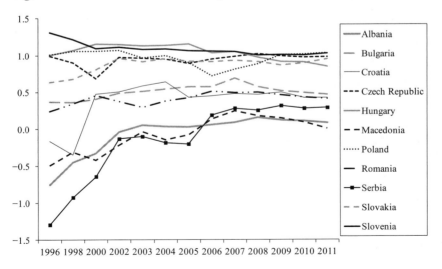

SOURCE: World Bank (2014).

Good Governance in Transition Economies 73

Figure 4.17 Political Stability in FSU and CEE Countries

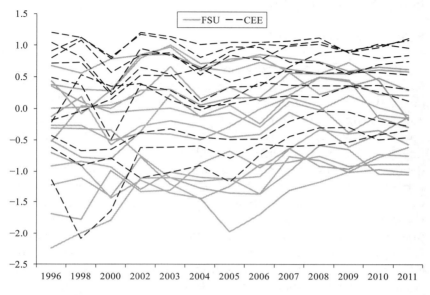

SOURCE: World Bank (2014).

Figure 4.18 Political Stability in FSU Countries

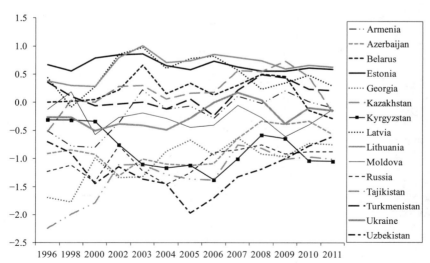

SOURCE: World Bank (2014).

ingly, CEE countries exhibit a general improvement in *political stability* over time (Figure 4.19).

Political Rights and Civil Liberties

Freedom House annually provides two composite governance-related measures for FSU, CEE, and other countries. As seen in Figure 4.20, CEE countries (darker) scored substantially higher than FSU countries (lighter) on both the political rights and civil liberties composite measures in 2012. Differences between FSU and CEE countries might be explained by different levels of commitment to bolstering democratic institutions, or by differences in the extent to which political leaders (national, regional, local) obtain and retain power. Differences might also be explained by the nature and scope of education and health care reforms, for example, or by policies targeted at immigration or freedom of the press. Such differences were driven in part by European Union membership requirements; most CEE countries have either joined or are candidate countries. Beyond the Baltic states, FSU countries have not been targeted for admission to the European Union.

Figure 4.19 Political Stability in CEE Countries

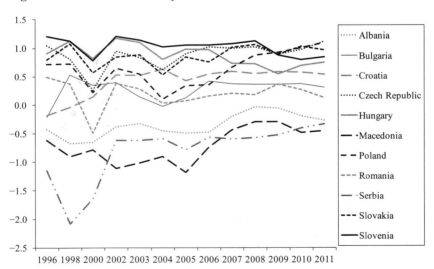

SOURCE: World Bank (2014).

Good Governance in Transition Economies 75

Figure 4.20 Freedom House Composite Scores, FSU and CEE Countries

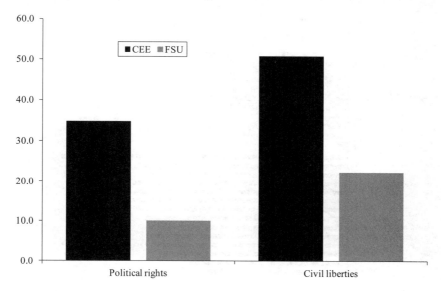

NOTE: Regional averages weighted by population.
SOURCE: Freedom House (2012).

Corruption Perceptions Index

Figure 4.21 presents the 2012 CPI scores for individual FSU countries (lighter) and CEE countries (darker). The construction of this index is explained on page 57. While in both groups only three countries have a score exceeding 50, among CEE countries there are eight that score over 40, in comparison to one of the FSU countries. Indeed, the Baltic republics (Estonia, Latvia, Lithuania) account for three of the top four FSU countries.

Index of Economic Freedom

The final governance measure considered here is the Index of Economic Freedom. Figure 4.22 presents the 2011 scores for FSU (lighter) and CEE (darker) countries; the higher the score, the more economic freedom.

Figure 4.21 Corruption Perceptions Index, FSU and CEE Countries

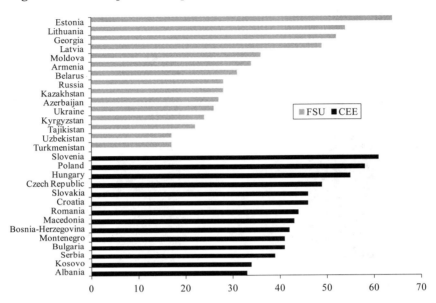

SOURCE: Transparency International (2013).

The pattern exhibited between FSU and CEE countries is clear, and it is invariant to the governance measure considered. Another perspective of the quality of governance in transition economies is provided by firm-level data. Such data not only are instrumental in undertaking empirical analyses of "state capture," but also to establish the time and financial costs imposed on firms by "bad" governance.

GOOD GOVERNANCE IN TRANSITION ECONOMIES: FIRMS' PERSPECTIVE AND EXPERIENCE

Empirical efforts and measures to assess good governance in transition economies tend to focus on aspects related to reducing or eliminating corruption. Similarly, studies of corruption in transition economies and elsewhere tend to focus on characteristics and policies of the

Good Governance in Transition Economies 77

Figure 4.22 Index of Economic Freedom, FSU and CEE Countries

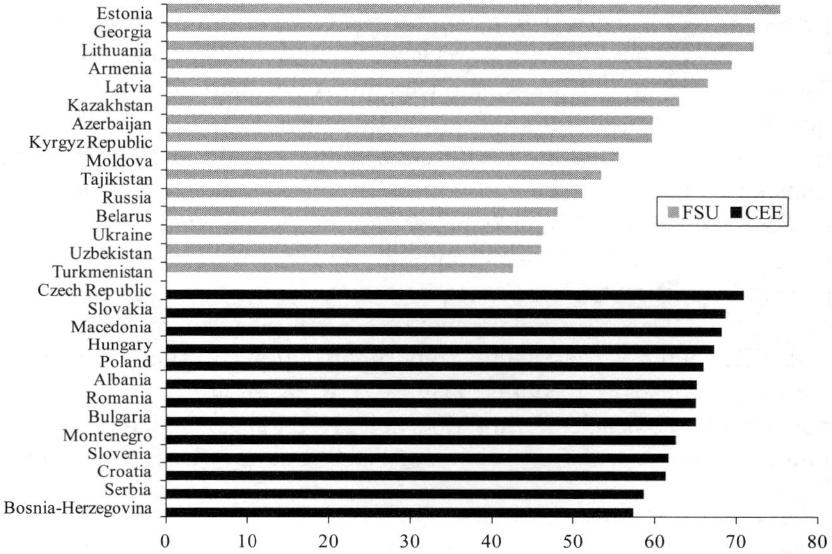

SOURCE: Heritage Foundation (2012).

state, with particular attention paid to the extent of state intervention in economic transactions and the degree of discretionary power wielded by bureaucrats (the macro perspective). An important source of information about the nature and scope of corruption, and thus the degree of good governance, comes from firms (the micro perspective). That is, the incidence and magnitude of corrupt activities that firms initiate (state capture) or are subjected to (grabbing hand), has direct consequences for whether governance is deemed "good" or "bad." Such data are invaluable in assessing the link between corporate governance and national governance (Hellman et al. 2000).

Among transition economies, firm-level data related to governance are collected by the Business Environment and Enterprise Performance Survey (BEEPS) (Brunetti et al. 1997, Hellman et al. 2000). Some of the questions relate to the efficacy of government institutions and policies,[24] while others focus more explicitly on interactions between firms and state.[25] The objective of this section is to summarize the most recent governance-related BEEPS data for FSU and CEE countries.

78 Linz

Hellman et al. (2000) use star charts for each country to report responses that relate to governance quality—firms' evaluation of the performance of major public institutions (central government, parliament, central bank, customs service, judiciary, police, and military). They provide similar information for firms' evaluation of the overall quality and efficiency of services provide by utilities (telephone, electricity, and water), public health care, education, the post office, and transportation/roads. Generally, firms in CEE countries tend to have higher evaluations (perceive better governance) than firms in FSU countries.[26] Here the focus is more narrow, on perception and experience of corruption among participating firms.

Figure 4.23 reports the percent of firms in FSU countries (lighter) and CEE countries (darker) that report corruption (bad governance) as the biggest obstacle to doing business,[27] while Figure 4.24 illustrates how big of an obstacle corruption is perceived to be. As seen in the two figures, while a greater proportion of FSU firms than CEE firms report

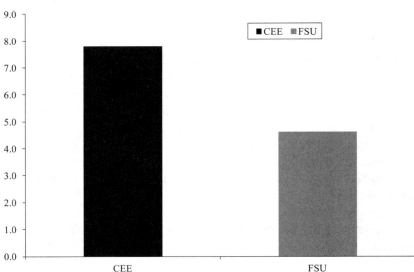

Figure 4.23 Percentage of Firms Listing Corruption as Biggest Obstacle, CEE and FSU Countries

SOURCE: World Bank Business Environment and Enterprise Performance Survey (BEEPS) data (World Bank 2015).

Figure 4.24 Percentage of Respondents Who Answered the Question "How Big of an Obstacle is Corruption?" in Each of Three Ways, CEE and FSU Countries

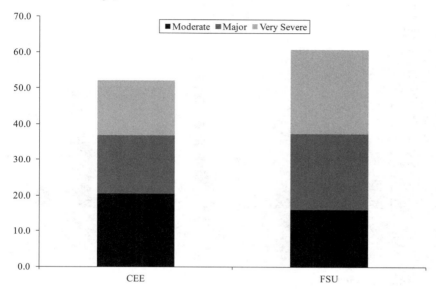

SOURCE: World Bank (2015).

that corruption is a very severe obstacle to doing business, corruption is less likely to be viewed by FSU firms as the biggest obstacle. In part this can be explained by the efficacy of the informal institutions in FSU countries (particularly Russia) that effectively guarantee the receipt of designated benefits associated with corrupt transactions. While costly to the firm, corruption is sustained by the culture of kinship and reciprocity, which promotes the informal institutions that enforce corrupt transactions, thereby reducing uncertainty associated with deriving benefits from such transactions.

Corrupt transactions frequently involve bribe payments. Figures 4.25 to 4.27 illustrate the type, frequency, and magnitude of bribe payments made by firms in FSU and CEE countries. Over 40 percent of the firms in the FSU sample report paying bribes for construction permits (see Figure 4.25), and they report paying, on average, more than 10 percent of the contract value (see Figure 4.27). Generally, a greater

Figure 4.25 Percentage of Firms That Said Bribes Were Requested/Expected for Nine Items, CEE and FSU Countries

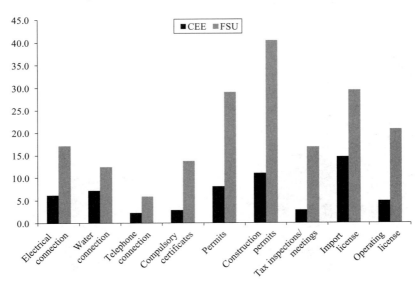

SOURCE: World Bank (2015).

percentage of firms in FSU countries (lighter) report making bribe payments for routine business activities (obtaining an operating license, utility connections, and the like) (see Figure 4.25), so it is not surprising to discover FSU firms reporting a higher incidence of interactions with government officials to make bribe payments (Figure 4.26). Nor is it surprising that a similar amount of time is spent by senior-level management in dealing with regulations (Figure 4.28). To put these figures into perspective, Figure 4.29 identifies the number of FSU and CEE firms in the respective samples that applied for required permits and utility connections in the previous two years, with Figure 4.30 illustrating the average number of days required to obtain a particular service.

Similarities between FSU and CEE countries in terms of general obstacles encountered are evident in Figure 4.31. Tax-related issues (see also Figure 4.32) and business licensing account for major sources of obstacles to doing business. The main difference between the two groups of countries involves labor regulations, which are perceived as more problematic in CEE countries than in FSU countries.

Figure 4.26 Bribe Frequency in Interactions with Government, CEE and FSU Countries (% of firms reporting)

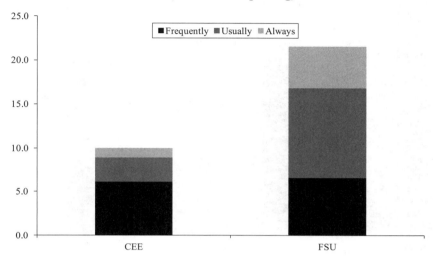

SOURCE: World Bank (2015).

Figure 4.27 Magnitude of Bribes and Kickbacks, CEE and FSU Countries

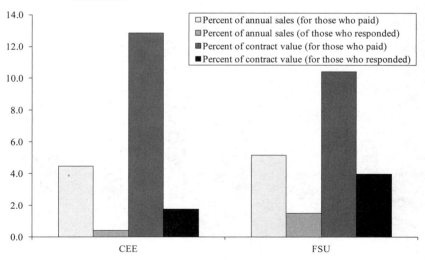

SOURCE: World Bank (2015).

82 Linz

Figure 4.28 Time Tax: Percentage of Senior Management Time Spent Dealing with Regulations, CEE and FSU Countries

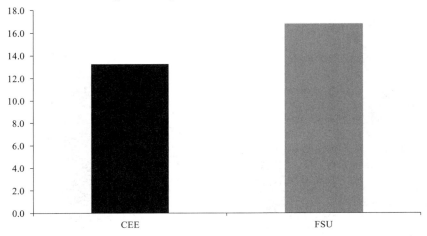

SOURCE: World Bank (2015).

Figure 4.29 Percentage of Firms That Have Applied for One of Six Things in the Past Two Years, CEE and FSU Countries

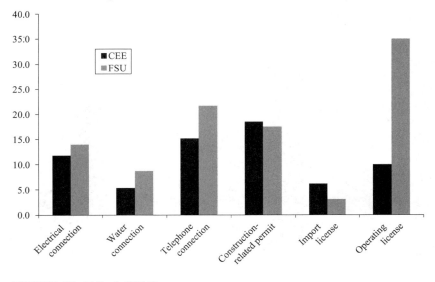

SOURCE: World Bank (2015).

Figure 4.30 Average Number of Days to Obtain One of Six Things, CEE and FSU Countries

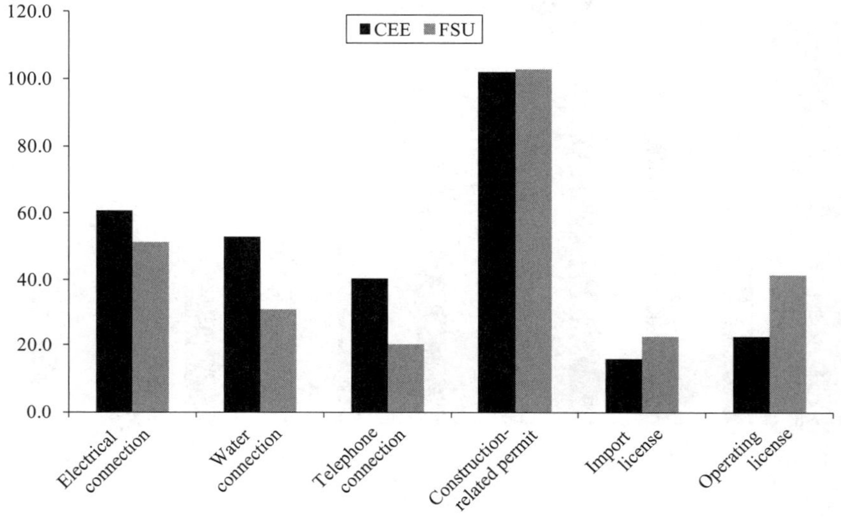

SOURCE: World Bank (2015).

SUMMARY AND CONCLUDING REMARKS

Governance involves the processes of decision making and decision implementation, and it takes place at the international, national, regional/local, and firm levels. Typically treated as a technical matter which can be solved by improved skill transfer, reorganizing structures, and providing additional resources, good governance is difficult to achieve. Good governance tends to emerge where there is bureaucratic competence, transparency, and predictability in the decision-making and implementation processes, and when fiscal sustainability and accountability become the norm.

Good governance is not an automatic outcome of democratization and liberalization in transition (former socialist) economies. As Bräutigam (2000) points out, good governance has some of the characteristics of public goods: everyone benefits, and since no one can be

84 Linz

Figure 4.31 Biggest Obstacles Facing Firms, CEE and FSU Countries

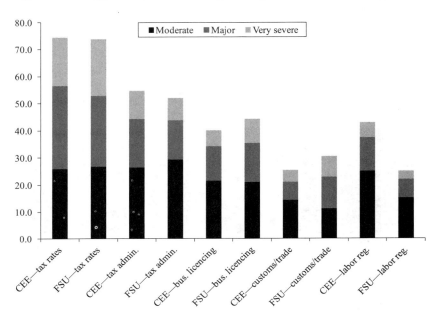

SOURCE: World Bank (2015).

excluded from the benefits, there is little incentive to pay (devote the resources necessary to promote good governance), and there may easily be obstacles to good governance among those who would lose their privileged position. Good governance is less frequently exhibited in FSU countries than in CEE countries. Partly this is explained by the institutional environment that existed in the countries before the socialist period began. Partly it is explained by the importance of kinship and reciprocity—i.e., the extensive reliance on social capital for completing routine transactions. Partly it is explained by initial conditions relating to corruption (bad governance): countries where corruption is high at the beginning of the transition process find it difficult to reduce or eliminate corruption over time.

International assistance does not guarantee good governance, even when different aspects of good governance are conditions of receiving aid. In countries where institutions are weak (legal or banking, for

Figure 4.32 Working Days Spent on One of Four Things, CEE and FSU Countries

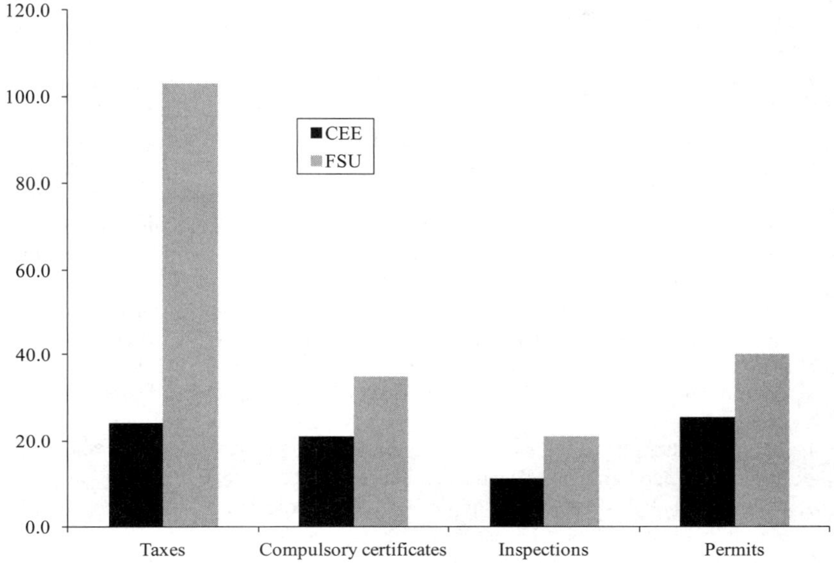

SOURCE: World Bank (2015).

example), international assistance may even contribute to "bad" governance: aid is diverted and corrupt individuals are not removed, local initiatives are "crowded out" as project managers and foreign experts oversee aid use, or countries embark on risky fiscal endeavors knowing that they likely will be bailed out, for instance.

While the contribution of good governance to economic, political, and social well being has been established, a few issues remain unresolved. How good does good governance need to be; is there a threshold level? At what level does good governance need to be exhibited: at the firm level, the local level, the national level, the international level—or at some combination of these? Resolving such questions will enable policymakers to more effectively implement good governance.

Notes

1. Williams and Siddique (2008) cite 85 studies that link governance quality to economic outcomes.
2. While the particular requirements may change over time or across countries, conditionality is necessary in order to document to taxpayers or donors that the money provided by the aid-granting agency was "well spent." At the same time, however, the governance literature points out the paradox that aid conditionality generates: aid to reduce poverty or promote social well-being requires good governance; countries where aid is most needed (i.e., where poverty conditions are most severe) exhibit limited ability to implement policies that promote characteristics of good governance. In a recent empirical study, Heckelman (2010) demonstrates that aid to transition economies did have positive consequences for some dimensions of governance (judicial, electoral) but not others (media independence).
3. European Bank for Reconstruction and Development (EBRD) data show that investment in the early 1990s was between 20 and 50 percent lower than pre-transition levels in former socialist economies (EBRD 2010).
4. While the literature is replete with studies that show that governance matters when it comes to economic performance, empirical studies that document causality provide mixed results (see, for example, Acemoglu, Johnson, and Robinson [2001]; Arndt and Oman [2006]; Glaeser et al. [2004]; and Mauro [1995]).
5. For a detailed description of the measures, see World Bank (2014).
6. For more information, see Freedom House (2012).
7. For more information, see Transparency International (2013).
8. For a detailed description of the methodology used to construct the Index of Economic Freedom, see Heritage Foundation (2012).
9. "Economic freedom" is defined as "the fundamental right of every human to control his or her own labor and property." See http://www.heritage.org/index/about.
10. For more information, see http://www.ebrd.com/pages/research/economics/data/beeps.shtml.
11. The Life in Transition Survey, conducted by the EBRD, collects information from individuals in transition economies about their perceptions and experience with corruption. See http://www.ebrd.com/pages/research/publications/special/transitionII.shtml.
12. Former Soviet Union or "FSU" countries include Armenia, Azerbaijan, Belarus, Estonia, Georgia, Kazakhstan, Krygyzstan, Latvia, Lithuania, Moldova, Russia, Tajikistan, Turkmenistan, Ukraine, and Uzbekistan. The Baltic republics (Estonia, Lavtia, and Lithuania), while grouped here as FSU, are sometimes included with CEE countries, because they chose not to join the post-Soviet Commonwealth of Independent States. Data are not always available for all countries in all years; hence, Figure 4.6 lists only 12 FSU countries, not 15.
13. CEE countries include Albania, Bosnia-Herzegovina, Bulgaria, Croatia, the Czech Republic, Hungary, Kosovo, Macedonia, Montenegro, Poland, Romania, Serbia, Slovakia, and Slovenia. Data are not always available for all countries in all years; hence, figures may show a varying number of CEE countries.

Good Governance in Transition Economies 87

14. *Voice and accountability* is designed to capture not only the extent to which individuals are able to express their opinions and ideas before, during, and after governmental decision making and implementation, but also their participation in making these decisions and the mechanism for imposing consequences associated with the decisions made.

15. *Control of corruption* is designed to capture "perceptions of the extent to which public power is exercised for private gain, including both petty and grand forms of corruption, as well as 'capture' of the state by elites and private interests" (taken from the WGI site http://info.worldbank.org/governance/wgi/index.aspx#faq).

16. In some instances, the objective is to influence the content of rules/regulations/laws (public-sector outcomes), and the activity or transaction is initiated by private-sector agents ("state capture"); in other instances, the objective of the activity or transaction is to use public-sector position for personal/private (financial) gain ("grabbing hand").

17. Knack (2006) describes a variety of corrupt interactions: between firms, between households, between firms and government individuals/agencies, between households and government individuals/agencies, and so forth.

18. Note that for Figures 4.2 through 4.19, the time intervals along the x axis change from two years to one year. This is because in 2003 Worldwide Governance Indicators data began to be gathered on a yearly rather than a biennial basis.

19. We note that comparative analyses based on governance measures derived from perceptions that involve longitudinal data are subject to two types of influences. First, differences over time may stem from changes in the composite measure: components added or subtracted, or new sources of information included. Second, events may occur at a point in time (election, financial crisis, public demonstrations, for example) that causes perceptions to change. Accounting for these two dimensions, as WGI does, allows for more accurate assessments of change.

20. According to Shlapentokh (2013), "hundreds of thousands of employees in private companies" receive not only their official salary but also a "salary in an envelope." This practice of companies (reporting wages below what was actually paid to their employees) allows firms to reduce their tax bill, and it is readily accepted by employees.

21. The WGI composite measure of *government effectiveness* is designed to capture "perceptions of the quality of public services, the quality of the civil service and the degree of its independence from political pressures, the quality of policy formulation and implementation, and the credibility of the government's commitment to such policies" (see http://info.worldbank.org/governance/wgi/index.aspx#faq).

22. *Regulatory quality* captures individuals' and firms' perceptions of government's ability to "formulate and implement sound policies and regulations that permit and promote private-sector development" (see http://info.worldbank.org/governance/wgi/index.aspx#faq).

23. The *political stability* composite measure is designed to capture "perceptions of the likelihood that the government will be destabilized or overthrown by unconstitutional or violent means, including politically motivated violence and terrorism" (see http://info.worldbank.org/governance/wgi/faq.htm).

88 Linz

24. Firms are asked to rate the quality of public services provided by central government, the judiciary (legal system), and such local authorities (institutions) as police and utilities, for example, in order to evaluate whether and which institutions impose obstacles to doing business.
25. Other questions focus on state intervention in firm operations (inspections, subsidies, bribes, etc.) and on firms' efforts to influence local or federal authorities (bribes, kickbacks, etc.).
26. Hellman et al. (2000) note issues related to perception bias and the likelihood that individuals in a particular country might be subject to similar kvetching (complaining) or kvelling (being overly optimistic). The survey design includes questions that can be verified or matched up with objective data (exchange rate variability and telephone infrastructure), thus Hellman et al. are able to undertake analyses to assess whether and where (which country) perception bias is problematic.
27. Sample selection by country took place in such a way as to generate a representative sample of firms. For discussion of the sample selection process, and the characteristics of the participating firms, see Hellman et al. (2000).

References

Abed, George T., and Hamid R. Davoodi. 2000. "Corruption, Structural Reforms, and Economic Performance in the Transition Economies." IMF Working Paper No. 00/132. Washington, DC: International Monetary Fund.

Acemoglu, Daron, Simon Johnson, and James A. Robinson. 2001. "The Colonial Origins of Comparative Development: An Empirical Investigation." *American Economic Review* 91(5): 1369–1401.

Aidis, Ruta, and Yuko Adachi. 2007. "Russia: Firm Entry and Survival Barriers." *Economic Systems* 31(4): 391–411.

Aidis, Ruta, Saul Estrin, and Tomasz M. Mickiewicz. 2008. "Institutions and Entrepreneurship Development in Russia: A Comparative Perspective." *Journal of Business Venturing* 23(6): 656–672.

Arndt, Christiane, and Charles Oman. 2006. *Uses and Abuses of Governance Indicators*. Development Centre Studies. Paris: Organisation for Economic Co-operation and Development. http://www.oecd.org/social/poverty/usesandabusesofgovernanceindicators.htm (accessed February 20, 2015).

Baniak, Andrzej, Jacek Cukrowski, and Jan Herczyñski. 2005. "On the Determinants of Foreign Direct Investment in Transition Economies." *Problems of Economic Transition* 48(2): 6–28.

Bardhan, Pranab, and Dilip Mookherjee. 2000. "Capture and Governance at Local and National Levels." *American Economic Review* 90(2): 135–139.

Berkowitz, Daniel, Katharina Pistor, and Jean-Francois Richard. 2003. "Economic Development, Legality, and the Transplant Effect." *European Economic Review* 47(1): 165–195.

Bevan, Alan A., and Saul Estrin. 2004. "The Determinants of Foreign Direct Investment into European Transition Economies." *Journal of Comparative Economics* 32(4): 775–787.

Bevan, Alan, Saul Estrin, and Klaus Meyer. 2004. "Foreign Investment Location and Institutional Development in Transition Economies." *International Business Review* 13(1): 43–64.

Bräutigam, Deborah. 2000. "Aid Dependence and Governance." EGDI Working Paper No. 2000:1. Stockholm: Ministry of Foreign Affairs, Department for International Development Cooperation, Expert Group on Development Issues. http://www.sti.ch/fileadmin/user_upload/Pdfs/swap/swap404 .pdf (accessed January 19, 2015).

Brunetti, Aymo, Gregory Kisunko, and Beatrice Wedner. 1997. "Institutional Obstacles to Doing Business: Region-by-Region Results from a Worldwide Survey of the Private Sector." Policy Research Working Paper No. 1323. Washington, DC: World Bank.

Craig, David, and Doug Porter. 2006. *Development beyond Neoliberalism? Governance, Poverty Reduction, and Political Economy.* New York: Routledge.

Dyker, David A. 2012. *Economic Policy Making and Business Culture: Why Is Russia So Different?* London: Imperial College Press.

European Bank for Reconstruction and Development (EBRD). 1999. *Transition Report: Ten Years of Transition.* London: European Bank for Reconstruction and Development.

———. 2010. *Transition Economies: Macroeconomic Indicators.* London: European Bank for Reconstruction and Development.

Freedom House. 2012. *Freedom House.* Washington, DC: Freedom House. https://freedomhouse.org/ (accessed April 3, 2015).

Frye, Timothy, and Andrei Shleifer. 1997. "The Invisible Hand and the Grabbing Hand." *American Economic Review* 87(2): 354–358.

Glaeser, Edward L., Rafael La Porta, Florencio Lopez-de-Silanes, and Andrei Shleifer. 2004. "Do Institutions Cause Growth?" *Journal of Economic Growth* 9(3): 271–303.

Hamadi, Fakhfakh, Ben Atitallah Rihab, and Ben Jedidia Lotfi. 2009. "Governance and Economic Growth in Transition Countries: A Reading in the Vision of the Institutional Theory." *International Journal of Economic Policy in Emerging Economies* 2(1): 1–22.

Heckelman, Jac C. 2010. "Aid and Democratization in the Transition Economies." *Kyklos* 63(4): 558–579.

Hellman, Joel S., Geraint Jones, and Daniel Kaufmann. 2002. "Far from

Home: Do Foreign Investors Import Higher Standards of Governance in Transition Economies?" Working paper. Washington, DC: World Bank. http://web.worldbank.org/archive/website00818/WEB/PDF/FARFROMH .PDF (accessed January 20, 2015).

Hellman, Joel S., Geraint Jones, Daniel Kaufmann, and Mark Schankerman. 2000. "Measuring Governance, Corruption, and State Capture: How Firms and Bureaucrats Shape the Business Environment in Transition Economies." World Bank Policy Research Working Paper No. 2312. London: European Bank for Reconstruction and Development; and Washington, DC: World Bank.

Heritage Foundation. 2012. *Methodology*. Washington, DC: Heritage Foundation. http://www.heritage.org/index/book/methodology (accessed April 3, 2015).

Johnson, Simon, Daniel Kaufmann, John McMillan, and Christopher Woodruff. 2000. "Why Do Firms Hide? Bribes and Unofficial Activity after Communism." *Journal of Public Economics* 76(3): 495–520.

Kaufmann, Daniel. 2005. "Myths and Realities of Governance and Corruption." In *Global Competitiveness Report 2005–06*. Geneva: World Economic Forum, pp. 81–98.

Kaufmann, Daniel, and Aart Kraay. 2007. "Governance Indicators: Where Are We, Where Should We Be Going?" World Bank Policy Research Working Paper No. 4370. Washington, DC: World Bank.

Kaufmann, Daniel, Aart Kraay, and Massimo Mastruzzi. 2010. "The Worldwide Governance Indicators: Methodology and Analytical Issues." World Bank Policy Research Working Paper No. 5430. Washington, DC: World Bank. http://ssrn.com/abstract=1682130 (accessed January 20, 2015).

Kaufmann, Daniel, Aart Kraay, and Pablo Zoido-Lobatón. 1999. "Governance Matters." World Bank Policy Research Working Paper No. 2196. Washington, DC: World Bank. http://info.worldbank.org/governance/wgi/pdf/govmatters1.pdf (accessed February 20, 2015).

Knack, Stephen. 2006. "Measuring Corruption in Eastern Europe and Central Asia: A Critique of the Cross-Country Indicators." World Bank Policy Research Working Paper No. 3968. Washington, DC: World Bank.

Lambsdorff, Johann Graf. 2007. *The Methodology of the Corruption Perceptions Index 2007*. Berlin: Transparency International; and Passau, Germany: University of Passau. http://www.icgg.org/downloads/CPI_2007 _Methodology.pdf (accessed January 21, 2015).

Ledeneva, Alena V. 1998. *Russia's Economy of Favours: Blat, Networking, and Informal Exchange*. New York: Cambridge University Press.

Levin, Mark, and Georgy Satarov. 2000. "Corruption and Institutions in Russia." *European Journal of Political Economy* 16(1): 113–132.

Mauro, Paolo. 1995. "Corruption and Growth." *Quarterly Journal of Economics* 110(3): 681–712.

Millar, James. 1996. "What's Wrong with the Mafiya Anyway? An Analysis of the Economics of Organized Crime in Russia." In *Economic Transition in Russia and the New States of Eurasia*, Bartlomiej Kaminski, ed. Armonk, NY: M. E. Sharpe, pp. 206–219.

Pistor, Katharina, Martin Raiser, and Stanislaw Gelfer. 2000. "Law and Finance in Transition Economies." *Economics of Transition* 8(2): 325–368.

Saisana, Michaela, and Andrea Saltelli. 2012. *Corruption Perceptions Index 2012: Statistical Assessment*. Luxembourg: European Commission, Joint Research Centre. http://publications.jrc.ec.europa.eu/repository/handle/JRC77239 (accessed January 21, 2015).

Santiso, Carlos. 2001. "Good Governance and Aid Effectiveness: The World Bank and Conditionality." *Georgetown Public Policy Review* 7(1): 1–22.

Shlapentokh, Vladimir. 2013. "Corruption, the Power of State and Big Business in Soviet and Post-Soviet Regimes." *Communist and Post-Communist Studies* 46(1): 147–158.

Shleifer, Andrei, and Robert W. Vishny. 1998. *The Grabbing Hand: Government Pathologies and Their Cures*. Cambridge, MA: Harvard University Press.

Steves, Franklin, and Alan Rousso. 2003. "Anti-Corruption Programmes in Post-Communist Transition Countries and Changes in the Business Environment, 1999–2002." EBRD Working Paper No. 85. London: European Bank for Reconstruction and Development.

Tonoyan, Vartuhi, Robert Strohmeyer, Mohsin Habib, and Manfred Perlitz. 2010. "Corruption and Entrepreneurship: How Formal and Informal Institutions Shape Small Firm Behavior in Transition and Mature Market Economies." *Entrepreneurship Theory and Practice* 34(5): 803–831.

Transparency International. 2013. *Transparency International*. Berlin: Transparency International. http://www.transparency.org (accessed April 3, 2015).

United Nations. 2013. *What Is Good Governance?* New York: United Nations Economic and Social Commission for Asia and the Pacific. New York: United Nations. http://www.unescap.org/sites/default/files/good-governance.pdf (accessed January 22, 2015).

Volkov, Vadim. 2000. "Organized Violence, Market Building, and State Formation in Post-Communist Russia." In *Economic Crime in Russia*, Alena V. Ledneva and Marina Kurkchiyan, eds. Boston: Kluwer Law, pp. 43–62.

Weiss, Thomas G. 2000. "Governance, Good Governance, and Global Governance: Conceptual and Actual Challenges." *Third World Quarterly* 21(5): 795–814.

Williams, Andrew, and Abu Siddique. 2008. "The Use (and Abuse) of Governance Indicators in Economics: A Review." *Economics of Governance* 9(2): 131–175.

Williamson, John. 1990. "What Washington Means by Policy Reform." In *Latin American Adjustment: How Much Has Happened?* John Williamson, ed. Washington, DC: Peterson Institute for International Economics, pp. 7–20.

World Bank. 2014. *Worldwide Governance Indicators.* Washington, DC: World Bank. http://info.worldbank.org/governance/wgi/index.aspx#home (accessed March 26, 2015).

———. 2015. *Beeps Data Portal.* Washington, DC: World Bank. http://beeps .prognoz.com/beeps/MultiHandler.ashx?slc=AboutBeeps (accessed April 3, 2015).

5

Governance Challenges in Education and Health Care in Developing Countries

Seema Jayachandran
Northwestern University

Ensuring that its citizens have access to high-quality schooling and health care is among a government's most important roles. Health and education—which enhance human capital—are widely believed to promote economic growth: schooling and health measures have both been linked to increased gross domestic product (GDP), and there are well-grounded reasons to believe that health and education boost worker productivity and, in turn, income. In addition, bolstering the health and education of children from poor families is one of the most powerful ways to break the intergenerational transmission of poverty and allow families to rise out of poverty. Moreover, health and education are basic human rights of every citizen, and governments are responsible for safeguarding these rights (United Nations 1948, Articles 25 and 26).

While there does exist private-sector provision of both health and education services in developing countries, the government is typically the main provider in these countries. In part, the government is filling in for a poorly developed private market, but there are also several reasons why governments have a natural role in these spheres, such as disease prevention or the externalities from having an educated population. Not only does the government account for a large share of the provision of services in the education and health care sectors, but education and health care also make up a large share of government spending. Health care and education account for over a third of the public-sector workforce in developing countries (Clements et al. 2010).

Unfortunately, governments in developing countries often do a poor job of delivering health care and education to their citizens. This

94 Jayachandran

chapter will focus on the ways in which governance challenges reduce the quality of education and health care provision in developing countries. In particular, I will consider ways in which corruption and poor oversight of the workforce reduce the efficacy of these sectors. I will document the causes, different manifestations, and extent of these problems. I will also discuss a range of promising policy solutions that have been adopted to address the problems, such as financial incentives, leveraging technological advancements to improve monitoring, information sharing through media outlets, and empowering stakeholders to improve accountability.

HEALTH AND EDUCATION INDICATORS IN DEVELOPING COUNTRIES

Despite the aforementioned reasons for governments to invest in the health of their populations, both health inputs and health outcomes tend to be much worse in poor countries than in rich countries. The highest neonatal and under-five mortality rates are found in developing countries. This finding is unsurprising, but what is staggering is the magnitude of the gap between rich and poor countries: under-five mortality rates in 2000 range from 241 deaths per 1,000 births to 4 deaths per 1,000 births (World Bank 2014). Health inputs exhibit the same pattern as health outcomes. For example, the child immunization rate is highly correlated with a country's GDP per capita.

Education levels in developing countries are also low. In such countries, 37 percent of the population aged 25 and over has no schooling, compared to 4 percent in developed countries. A similar pattern is seen in the percentage of people with a secondary-school education or higher—27 percent in developing countries compared to 68 percent in developed countries (Barro and Lee 2001).

The *quality* of available health and education services and not simply low take-up is at the heart of the problem. For example, those who do attend school in developing countries often receive a low-quality education. Schoellman (2012) uses U.S. census data to estimate returns to schooling for foreign-educated immigrants working in the United States. By comparing immigrants who were educated in, say, Nigeria to those educated in France, he calculates how much money an extra year of schooling in Nigeria is worth in the U.S. labor market compared to an extra year of schooling in France. This estimate provides a metric of school quality in the different origin countries. When this proxy for school quality is compared with GDP per capita, there is a strong positive relationship between a country's GDP and school quality. Schoellman finds that differences in education quality are as important as differences in years of schooling when decomposing the variation in human capital accumulation across countries.

Poor-quality education also negatively affects school enrollment rates: parents have less of a reason to send their children to a school where they are not learning, and students have less interest in attending a school where they are not engaged. An eye-opening report featured interviews with parents in India about their children's schooling (PROBE 1999). In 8 percent of the cases where boys were withdrawn from school and 18 percent of the cases where girls were withdrawn from school, parents reported that the reason for their having taken their child out of school was poor teaching. Poor quality also stops parents from ever enrolling their children in school in the first place for 8 percent of boys and 1 percent of girls. One mother in the state of Madhya Pradesh explained why she had never sent her daughter, Rukmini, to school: "If we send the girl to school, we have to pay a labourer to replace her, and the girl learns nothing. What do we gain? See this other child who is in class 5. She knows nothing. My son Parkash studied till class 6—he knows nothing" (ibid., p. 27).

The quality of health care is also often inadequate. One dimension of quality is the level of effort health care providers exert. A study in urban India investigated this aspect of quality by comparing providers' actions in a hypothetical test environment to observed practices in the clinic (Das and Hammer 2005). The study interviewed and observed a representative sample of both public and private health care providers. The health care providers participated in "vignettes" in which trained research staff acted out various hypothetical health scenarios. Doctors were scored on the questions they asked the "patients," diagnosis, and recommended treatment. Vignette scores were used to assign a competence score to each provider—how much the provider knew. One month after this exercise, research staff observed providers in their actual practice for a full working day and scored each patient interaction based on the amount of time the health care provider spent with the patient, questions the provider asked the patient, examinations, and recommendations. These scores were then compared to the vignette scores to create a measure of provider effort. A main finding is that providers' actual performance was well short of their potential performance: providers knew what to do but did not do it in practice. Among providers with a medical degree, those in the private sector completed only 60 percent of the activities they knew to be important, and those in the public sector completed only 33 percent. Thus, the problem was particularly acute for public health care providers. Differences in effort were most salient in poor neighborhoods, where patients appeared to be better off visiting private providers rather than public providers, despite the fact that public providers were more qualified and presumably less expensive.

GOVERNANCE PROBLEMS IN THE HEALTH AND EDUCATION SECTORS

As described above, in many cases governments in developing countries are failing to provide high-quality health care and education. One important factor is poor governance, which I define as the inefficient management and use of the available resources, often owing to malfeasance or shirking by government employees. While governance does not account for all of the problems in the health care and education sectors—the available financial and human resources are often very limited—it plays a central role. The governance problems run the gamut, from graft and bribery to absenteeism and indolence among employees.

Graft

Perhaps the simplest type of governance problem is theft of financial resources. A well-known World Bank study in Uganda "followed the money" to document the extent of graft by local bureaucrats (Reinikka and Svensson 2004). The central government in Uganda disbursed education grants to individual schools based on the number of students enrolled. By tracking the disbursements and then the amount received by the schools, the study found that schools received on average only 20 percent of the amount they were entitled to. The median percentage of the federal grant received was 0 percent! The missing money apparently was captured by local bureaucrats and was not reallocated to other public uses but rather was stolen for personal use. While this is just one specific example, it is representative of what is widely believed to be a prevalent problem: bureaucrats skim off some of the money that should be spent to buy supplies, maintain facilities, and pay teachers and health care workers.

Informal Payments

Government employees can also enrich themselves by demanding "informal payments" for services that should be rendered for free or at a specified rate. Essentially, the government employee is extracting a bribe in exchange for performing a service that he is contractually obligated to provide even if this bribe is not paid. Lewis (2007) reviews the literature on informal payments in the health sector and highlights the prevalence of the practice across countries for basic services such as admission to the hospital or receipt of subsidized medications. She reports on a survey in Bangalore, India, by Gopakumar (1998) that found that 51 percent of community members surveyed had paid bribes in government hospitals, while 89 percent had paid bribes in hospitals in small towns. In one of the more egregious examples cited, individuals reported having to pay bribes to nurses in maternity homes so that mothers could see their newborns.

A related phenomenon is seen in schooling, though perhaps less frequently. In crowded classes, teachers sometimes ask parents to pay a fee so their child can sit in the front of the classroom and get more attention. It is also not unheard of for a teacher to demand payment in order to advance the student to the next grade or give high marks.

Absenteeism

Worker absenteeism is a major challenge in both the health care and the education sectors: employees simply do not show up to work. Banerjee, Deaton, and Duflo (2004) document absence rates in health care facilities using survey data from public and private medical providers, as well as traditional healers, in a poor, rural district of India. In the public sector, absence rates were verified by weekly, in-person visits (random spot checks) to public health facilities over the course of one year. Subcenters and aid posts (the lowest-tier health facilities) suffer from the highest rates of absenteeism: those performing the spot checks found that 56 percent of facilities were closed during normal working hours. In contrast, primary and community health centers (PHCs and CHCs) were closed only 3 percent of the time when the spot checkers showed up. However, when facilities *were* open, both subcenters and PHCs/CHCs were understaffed: the fraction of allocated medical staff found during a visit averaged 55 percent for subcenters and 64 percent for PHCs/CHCs. One perilous consequence of this low-quality government care is that it drives patients to private care. In rural India, private health care providers are often severely underqualified. In the area studied by Banerjee, Deaton, and Duflo, 82 percent of private providers reported that they had no medical training whatsoever.

This pattern of absenteeism is supported by cross-country data from Chaudhury et al. (2006). Survey teams in six countries made two to three in-person visits to a (nearly) nationally representative sample of primary schools and primary health centers. On average, the education sector suffered from an absence rate of 19 percent, while the health sector had an absence rate of 35 percent. Absence rates declined as per capita income increased, especially in the education sector.

Shirking

The absence rates described above may understate the severity of just how poor the provision of service may be, in that providers who are present may not actually be working. Chaudhury et al. (2006) found that in India teachers who were present during spot checks were actually teaching only 45 percent of the time. Even this statistic may overestimate effort, as teachers were counted as teaching in instances where they were only keeping the class in order and not actually teaching. Data from secondary schools in Nepal show a similar, though less severe, pattern: 18 percent of teachers failed to teach for the entire class period (Jayachandran 2014).

Perverse Incentives as a Contributing Factor

Government workers' lack of effort may merely stem from the lack of positive incentives to work hard, but in some cases there are perverse incentives that reward teachers or health care workers for poor performance. Jayachandran (2014) studies the prevalent phenomenon of after-school tutoring in government schools in which schoolteachers provide for-profit tutoring to their own students outside of the normal school day. The possibility of extra income from tutoring may incentivize teachers to teach less material during the normal school day, thereby increasing the likelihood that their students will need to attend tutoring. Jayachandran uses data from a national survey in Nepal to investigate the effect of a secondary school offering tutoring on teacher effort and student academic achievement. Students in private and public schools were asked to report whether they received tutoring, whether or not their teacher taught for the entire class period, and other subjective information on teacher performance. These data were then linked with students' scores on the national secondary-school exam. After-school tutoring in public schools was found to reduce the likelihood that teachers taught for the entire class period by 7 percentage points, a significant reduction. Less teaching translated into a lower student performance on the secondary-school exam. This finding did not carry over to private schools, which is not surprising when one considers that private schools, unlike public schools, face a financial hit if they teach inadequately during the regular school day, since they will lose students and hence school-fee revenues. The students hurt most by this practice of "self-dealing" are those whose families are too poor to afford tutoring; these students are taught less during school than the teacher could have feasibly covered, but are not able to learn the missed material by taking the tutoring classes.

Reverse or perverse incentives are also found in the health care sector. Doctors whose wages are linked to the number of medicines, tests, or procedures they recommend are more likely to prescribe unneeded treatments. This phenomenon is widespread in China, where the antibiotic prescription rate is almost double that of other countries. Doctors are incentivized to overprescribe by their hospitals, which make money from setting higher prices for certain drugs, and also by pharmaceutical companies, which provide doctors with bonuses to increase sales.

A randomized audit study showed that doctors were significantly less likely to prescribe antibiotics to patients who signaled they had some knowledge that antibiotics might not be needed to treat their symptoms (39 percent of such cases received antibiotics) compared to patients that did not (64 percent of such cases received antibiotics). Patients who demonstrated knowledge about antibiotics were also less likely to be prescribed multiple drugs or more expensive drugs (Currie, Lin, and Zhang 2011).

In both of these examples—tutoring and overprescription of drugs—the problem is worse than bribery. Not only are government workers extracting money from citizens, but here, in the pursuit of additional money for themselves, government workers intentionally provide what they know to be lower-quality service, be it less teaching during class or unnecessary medicines.

Why Do These Governance Problems Exist?

There are fundamental reasons why governance problems are severe in developing countries and are pervasive in the health care and education sectors. Many other government services are based primarily in cities or towns, but schools and health clinics are located throughout a country. That geographic spread is one underlying reason that monitoring workers is difficult. Many schools and health posts are located in remote villages, causing a twofold problem. First, poor-quality roads and inadequate public transportation make it difficult for government workers to reach their place of work. Second, these same conditions also hinder supervisors or auditors from traveling to conduct spot checks and worker evaluations. Thus, there is often little monitoring of the performance of government workers.

Another contributing factor is that government workers earn a low salary by worldwide standards (though they are often well paid relative to their skill group in their countries). Many health care and education workers moonlight at other jobs to supplement their income. Workers with multiple jobs are more likely to be absent if their jobs have conflicting schedules, and they may also exert less effort—for example, a teacher might have less time to prepare a lesson.

A third important factor that exacerbates these issues is that consumers are less able to monitor service provision and enforce high quality than they are in wealthier countries. Parents with limited education may lack the ability to gauge what their child is learning in school or how their local school's performance compares to other schools in the region (Dizon-Ross 2014). Similarly, patients tend to have little knowledge of whether or not a health care provider is performing the needed tests, asking the appropriate questions, and making an accurate diagnosis. Even when stakeholders are aware that services are inadequate, they may not have sufficient leverage or social standing within the community to hold providers accountable. It is much more likely that a parent in a developing country has less education and status compared to her child's teacher than would be the case in developed countries, simply because teachers have a higher position in the society-wide distribution of schooling attainment in developing countries than in developed countries.

Finally, it is often difficult to fire government employees, so governments have few tools to enforce job requirements and punish shirkers even when they are able to monitor workers adequately and would like to improve the effort level of the workforce.

Beyond Governance: Limited Resources

It is important to note that there are many factors other than governance challenges that contribute to poor health and education outcomes in developing countries. The amount of available government revenue is lower, which means fewer resources for education and health care. This translates into larger class sizes and inadequate teaching aids or faulty hospital equipment and lack of medicine. Infrastructure is also poor, with many facilities lacking water and electricity. These other problems may very well exacerbate the governance challenges described above. In an analysis of cross-country data, teacher absence rates fall by 2.7 percentage points with a one standard deviation increase in an index measuring school infrastructure. A similar pattern is observed in the health care sector, where the availability of potable water at the facility significantly decreases the absence rates of health care workers (Chaudhury et al. 2006).

SOME PROMISING APPROACHES TO ADDRESSING GOVERNANCE CHALLENGES

Governments are typically ineffective at monitoring workers and enforcing performance standards. While these are difficult problems to overcome, there has been progress recently through innovative approaches by governments to incentivize good performance, monitor their workers, and empower citizens to monitor government workers.

Incentive Schemes

A basic but powerful idea in economics is that an employer can align workers' incentives with the employer's objectives by means of pay for performance. Recent pilot programs have shown the benefits of incentive schemes in improving teacher performance and reducing absenteeism in schools. A nonprofit foundation collaborated with the state government in Andhra Pradesh, India, to conduct a randomized evaluation of performance pay for teachers in rural primary schools. Two schemes were assessed: group bonuses tied to school performance and individual bonuses tied to teacher performance. The schemes were evaluated over the course of two years, during which student performance was assessed at the end of each school year (Muralidharan and Sundararaman 2011). Bonuses were awarded if average test scores (either for the school or for the individual teacher) increased by at least 5 percent. The researchers evaluating the program conducted unannounced spot checks to measure student and teacher attendance as well. The program, including both schemes, significantly improved student performance: scores in language increased by 0.17 standard deviations, and math scores increased by 0.27 standard deviations. As judged against other policy innovations in education, these were impressively large impacts on student test scores. Muralidharan and Sundararaman conclude that the improvements in test scores were due to increased teacher effort rather than improved teacher or student attendance. An innovative feature of the study is that student performance was measured in subjects such as science and social science, where performance was not factored into teacher pay. One concern about teacher incentive pay is that teachers might "teach to the test," and other types of learning might suffer. In this case, performance in all subjects improved, presumably because the teacher put in more effort across the board, or because better student learning in math and language had spillover benefits to other subjects such as science and social science.

Duflo, Hanna, and Ryan (2012), whose study is discussed in more detail below, analyze another incentive program in schools and find that linking incentives for teachers to their attendance improved student test scores.

Technology

A second potential solution to shortcomings in the health care and education sectors is to use technology to improve staff monitoring. High rates of absenteeism may be due, in part, to the fact that there is no accountability for providers. By leveraging advances in technology, it may be possible to reduce some of the barriers that prevent governments from actively monitoring attendance and performance. A nongovernmental organization (NGO) in India attempted to reduce teacher absences by using cameras to document attendance. Teachers were given a digital camera with a tamper-proof date and time stamp and were instructed to have a student take one photograph at the beginning of the school day and one at the end of the school day. To be considered valid, photographs had to be taken at least five hours apart, and both photographs had to have at least eight children pictured with the teacher. A randomized evaluation assessed the effectiveness of this program using data from unscheduled spot checks by the survey team, teacher photos, and student test scores (Duflo, Hanna, and Ryan 2012). The program was found to significantly reduce absence rates in camera schools (where the rate fell to 21 percent) compared to noncamera schools (where the absence rate was 42 percent). Student test scores in schools with cameras were also significantly higher (by 0.17 standard deviations), which led to more students from these schools passing competency exams to continue their schooling. This positive impact on student achievement is an important result because it indicates that teachers did not "game the system" and simply show up to work but not teach. Rather, the incentive to show up to work increased their teaching and, in turn, student learning.

Even more advanced technology is now being leveraged in the health care sector. The state government in Karnataka, India, recently launched something known as the Integrated Medical Information and Disease Surveillance System (IMIDSS), in which biometric devices record health care worker attendance using thumbprints. Attendance data is sent in real time to monitors in government headquarters using cellular or radio networks. This monitoring is linked to both incentives and penalties for the health care workers. A randomized evaluation of the effectiveness of this program finds that it both increases health care worker attendance and improves patient health outcomes (Dhaliwal and Hanna 2014).

Citizen Empowerment

Improving citizens' knowledge can be an important first step toward increasing government accountability. Media outlets offer a means to increase citizens' awareness. This approach was used by the central government in Uganda in response to learning that grants for schools were being siphoned off by local government officials, as discussed above. Prior to the intervention, the average school in the sample received only 24 percent of the grant money to which it was entitled. In an attempt to increase accountability, the Ugandan government launched a newspaper campaign to disseminate information to parents and teachers about the federal grants their local school was entitled to. Two public-expenditure tracking surveys administered six years apart, one pre- and one postintervention, were used to assess the effectiveness of the campaign. Data indicated that head teachers' knowledge of the grant programs significantly increased with proximity to a newspaper outlet, both in terms of the funding rules and the timing of the release of funds (Reinikka and Svensson 2005).[1] Increased knowledge led to more money reaching schools. With each standard deviation increase in head teachers' knowledge of entitlements, the funds received by the school increased by an average of 44 percent. In addition to reducing the capture of public funds by larcenous local officials, the campaign had a positive effect on student enrollment: A one-standard-deviation increase in the school's share of received funding resulted in an increase of 297 more students per school.

While citizens are aware of their personal experiences, there is often no way for them to measure quality of services in terms of aggregate outcomes in the community. An intervention in Uganda in 2004 aimed to empower citizens by providing such aggregated information to the community, in this case about health care. Rather than using mass media, this intervention brought together local government health care workers and community members to disseminate the information and discuss how to improve health care provision. The program was found to have significantly improved health care delivery and health outcomes (Björkman and Svensson 2009). First, researchers surveyed both community members and health care providers to collect data on health outcomes (verified by medical records when possible), health facility characteristics, and provider performance. This information was used to create a unique report card for each village health care facility, and the information on the village's report card was presented at community meetings by local NGOs. These report cards were used as a conversation starting point for community representatives and providers to develop action plans for improving service delivery and monitoring. The randomized evaluation of the intervention found that health care service delivery and health outcomes improved in several significant ways: Average waiting time decreased by 12 minutes, from 131 to 119 minutes, and there was a 0.56 standard deviation increase in the index used to measure facility conditions (cleanliness of floors, walls, furniture, and so forth). Absence rates among service providers also declined. Most strikingly, the intervention resulted in several improved health outcomes such as child weight and child survival.

An important cautionary note is in order, specifically about community information interventions, but also more broadly about the universal applicability of any type of solution. While the results of the Ugandan community intervention are promising, other community empowerment programs have been found to be less successful. Kremer and Holla (2009) outline the null findings of evaluations in two different countries that aimed to empower education stakeholders. One intervention in India sought to improve the performance of community monitoring committees for schools, which had been ineffective from the outset. Survey results showed that few households were aware of these committees. Tests were also administered to children to assess school quality. Results indicated that parents had an inaccurate understanding of how much their children were learning. To solve this problem, officials fashioned an intervention that was aimed at informing the community about the following areas: school performance, state-mandated school requirements, funding, and the responsibilities of the preexisting monitoring committees. Despite the fact that almost 30 percent of households attended these meetings, monitoring committees in villages that received the intervention were no more effective than committees in villages with no intervention. Teacher and student absences were also unchanged.

Two programs in Kenya also targeted community monitoring bodies for schools. Of note, while the majority of teachers in Kenyan schools are directly employed by the government, schools or monitoring committees sometimes hire contract teachers to work with the government-employed teachers. The first intervention attempted to empower these committees by providing prizes which committees could bestow on teachers to incentivize them and by facilitating meetings between parents, committee members, and civil-service teachers. Results echo those of the empowerment intervention in India—there was no effect on teacher absence or student achievement.

The second program in Kenya aimed to improve committee monitoring of contract teacher attendance. While the program did not change attendance among contract teachers (which was already relatively high), the program did somewhat improve the attendance of civil-service teachers, though the results were not statistically significant. Despite the fact that there was no significant change in teacher attendance, the program did improve student attendance and performance in the classrooms of civil-service teachers.

Thus, while the approach of citizen empowerment had remarkable impacts on the health care sector in Uganda, the same approach was relatively ineffective on the education sector in Kenya and India. One hopes that policymakers, NGOs, and researchers will go back to the drawing board and devise other approaches to solve the problem of poor-quality education in these latter settings where the first attempt failed. These examples serve as a reminder that there is no one-size-fits-all solution, and that the process of improving governance in developing countries will be laborious and often frustrating.

CONCLUSION

The majority of funding in the health care and education sectors is spent on provider salaries. For example, 80 percent of India's health care budget is dedicated to provider compensation (Das and Hammer 2005). A similar pattern is observed in education budgets, where, on average, 75 percent of funding goes toward teacher salaries in developing countries (Kremer and Holla 2009). Thus, improving the quality of health and education hinges on improving the performance of the workforce.

There are several basic features of poor countries that create governance challenges in monitoring public workers and incentivizing them to perform well. Thus, governance problems are pervasive in the education and health care sectors and act as a barrier to high-quality education and health care services. The lack of high-quality education and health care services in turn obstructs educational attainment and good health outcomes. While no panacea exists, innovative solutions are being developed and tested: redesigning incentive schemes, using technology to monitor workers, and empowering citizens with information, often disseminated through mass media. There is still much work to be done to solve these governance problems, but the problems are well worth tackling given the importance of human capital for reducing poverty and promoting economic growth in developing countries.

Notes

I can be reached at the Department of Economics at Northwestern University and by e-mail at seema@northwestern.edu. I am grateful to Jaye Stapleton for excellent research assistance.

1. A "head teacher" in Uganda is similar to what in the United States or Great Britain would be called a "headmaster," except that a head teacher often has regular teaching duties in addition to part-time administrative ones.

108 Jayachandran

References

Banerjee, Abhijit, Angus Deaton, and Esther Duflo. 2004. "Health Care Delivery in Rural Rajasthan." *Economic and Political Weekly* 39(9): 944–949.

Barro, Robert J., and Jong-Wha Lee. 2001. "International Data on Educational Attainment: Updates and Implications." *Oxford Economic Papers* 53(3): 541–563.

Björkman, Martina, and Jakob Svensson. 2009. "Power to the People: Evidence from a Randomized Field Experiment on Community-Based Monitoring in Uganda." *Quarterly Journal of Economics* 124(2): 735–769.

Chaudhury, Nazmul, Jeffrey Hammer, Michael Kremer, Karthik Muralidharan, and F. Halsey Rogers. 2006. "Missing in Action: Teacher and Health Worker Absence in Developing Countries." *Journal of Economic Perspectives* 20(1): 91–116.

Clements, Benedict, Sanjeev Gupta, Izabela Karpowicz, and Shamsuddin Tareq. 2010. *Evaluating Government Employment and Compensation.* Technical Notes and Manuals 10/15. Washington, DC: International Monetary Fund, Fiscal Affairs Department.

Currie, Janet, Wanchuan Lin, and Wei Zhang. 2011. "Patient Knowledge and Antibiotic Abuse: Evidence from an Audit Study in China." *Journal of Health Economics* 30(5): 933–949.

Das, Jishnu, and Jeffrey Hammer. 2005. "Money for Nothing: The Dire Straits of Medical Practice in Delhi, India." World Bank Policy Research Working Paper No. 3669. Washington, DC: World Bank.

Dhaliwal, Iqbal, and Rema Hanna. 2014. "Deal with the Devil: The Successes and Limitations of Bureaucratic Reform in India." NBER Working Paper No. 20482. Cambridge, MA: National Bureau of Economic Research.

Dizon-Ross, Rebecca. 2014. "Parents' Perceptions and Children's Education: Experimental Evidence from Malawi." Unpublished working paper, Massachusetts Institute of Technology, Cambridge, MA.

Duflo, Esther, Rema Hanna, and Stephen P. Ryan. 2012. "Incentives Work: Getting Teachers to Come to School." *American Economic Review* 102(4): 1241–1278.

Gopakumar, K. 1998. "Citizen Feedback Surveys to Highlight Corruption in Public Services: The Experience of Public Affairs Centre, Bangalore." Unpublished working paper, Transparency International, Berlin.

Jayachandran, Seema. 2014. "Incentives to Teach Badly? After-School Tutoring in Developing Countries." *Journal of Development Economics* 108(May): 190–205.

Kremer, Michael, and Alaka Holla. 2009. "Improving Education in the Developing World: What Have We Learned from Randomized Evaluations?" *Annual Review of Economics* 1(1): 513–542.

Lewis, Maureen. 2007. "Informal Payments and the Financing of Health Care in Developing and Transition Countries." *Health Affairs* 26(4): 984–997.

Muralidharan, Karthik, and Venkatesh Sundararaman. 2011. "Teacher Performance Pay: Experimental Evidence from India." *Journal of Political Economy* 119(1): 39–77.

PROBE Team in association with the Centre for Development Economics (PROBE). 1999. *Public Report on Basic Education in India*. New Delhi: Oxford University Press.

Reinikka, Ritva, and Jakob Svensson. 2004. "Local Capture: Evidence from a Central Government Transfer Program in Uganda." *Quarterly Journal of Economics* 119(2): 679–705.

———. 2005. "Fighting Corruption to Improve Schooling: Evidence from a Newspaper Campaign in Uganda." *Journal of the European Economic Association* 3(2–3): 259–267.

Schoellman, Todd. 2012. "Education Quality and Development Accounting." *Review of Economic Studies* 79(1): 388–417.

United Nations. 1948. *The Universal Declaration of Human Rights*. New York: United Nations. http://www.un.org/en/documents/udhr/index.shtml#atop (accessed November 13, 2014).

World Bank. 2014. *Mortality Rate, Under-5 (per 1,000 live births)*. Washington, DC: World Bank. http://data.worldbank.org/indicator/SH.DYN.MORT (accessed November 5, 2014).

6
Governance Problems and Priorities for Local Climate Adaptation and Poverty Alleviation

Stephen C. Smith
George Washington University

This chapter begins by reviewing the encouraging progress that has been made against poverty over the past three decades, but then it considers some reasons for concern as to why further progress may be difficult. Two key constraints are environmental stress and poor governance. Governance failures slow economic growth and often particularly affect the poor; they may also lead to violent conflict, with particular harm to people living in poverty. Environmental degradation can cause poverty and indirectly lead to conflict. Adaptation on the parts of both government and the private sector is an essential response to climate change, and people who successfully adapt may also be less vulnerable to violence, as well as less likely to provoke conflict. But without good governance, actions people take to try to adapt to climate change may in themselves trigger conflict. Thus, it is essential to improve governance for adaptation, both in terms of government's overall planned adaptation responses and in its facilitation of successful, harmonious, and autonomous adaptation in the private sector and civil society.

PROGRESS AGAINST POVERTY: THE GLASS IS HALF FULL

Clear Progress on Poverty since 1980

Since 1980, the fraction of the world's population living on less than $1.25 a day has fallen from over 40 percent down to just over 20 percent. Indeed, given that some have put forward higher estimates of the number living in poverty in China in 1980, the global incidence of extreme poverty in that year may have been closer to 50 percent. The World Bank reports that its Millennium Development Goals (MDGs) target of halving the fraction of people that were living in poverty in 1990 (about 40 percent that year) by the year 2015 had already been achieved by 2010 (United Nations 2012). Moreover, 6 of the 10 fastest-growth economies since 2005 have been in Africa, the region with the greatest fraction in poverty (World Bank 2013). On the other hand, with the commodity price declines coinciding with the growth slowdown in China, the sustainability of this higher growth level is called into question.

There has also been impressive improvement in most health indicators (Smith 2005). Life expectancy has risen, under-five mortality has fallen, and maternal mortality has been reduced. Education enrollments have also risen, along with basic literacy. While it remains in dispute as to whether incomes are converging globally, there is little doubt that there has been convergence in education and health levels in recent decades, and the international convergence of health and of education are mutually reinforcing (Sab and Smith 2002; UNDP 2012).

Improved governance is foundational to successful development (North 1990), and there has been an impressive spread of democracy and of government transparency (UNDP 2012).

Remaining Poverty Challenges

But some of the important MDG targets—such as halving world hunger—will not be achieved by the 2015 deadline (World Bank 2011).

There is a growing concentration of poverty in conflict-affected states and regions with deteriorating environments—precisely where progress is most difficult (World Bank 2010a, 2011; World Resources Institute et al. 2011).

And environmental decay is proceeding at a pace few had predicted 20 years ago. Among other things, this is posing serious threats to the natural-resource-based livelihoods that so many of the global poor depend upon (World Resource Institute et al. 2011).

Thus, much remains to be done—although the glass is half full, it remains half empty.

Governance Problems and Priorities for Local Climate Adaptation 113

About 1.2 billion people currently subsist on less than $1.25 a day (the adjusted level, still known as the "dollar a day" level), and about 2.7 billion—nearly two-fifths of the world's population—live on less than $2 a day. At least 300 million people live in chronic extreme poverty (Todaro and Smith 2011, Chapter 5).

Unfortunately, sub-Saharan Africa has shown far less progress than other developing regions. While the fraction living in poverty has gone down somewhat in the past decade, the head count (number) of individuals living in poverty rose dramatically in the 1981–2010 period, from about 205 million to about 414 million. The concentration of poverty may make it more difficult to redress. In most countries, the poverty gap has gone down along with the poverty head count. But between 1981 and 2010, the average income of the extremely poor hardly increased in sub-Saharan Africa, remaining near an appalling 70 cents per person per day (World Bank 2013).

This stagnation is closely connected to the lack of a sustained Green Revolution in Africa. Sub-Saharan Africa has very little irrigation, a factor that worsens constraints as climate change accelerates. World Bank research reveals that in 2007 only about 4 percent of farmland in sub-Saharan Africa was irrigated. Africa's risky, rain-fed agriculture contrasts with 39 percent irrigation incidence in South Asia and 29 percent incidence in East Asia and the Pacific. Moreover, despite progress, more than three-quarters of cereal-producing farmland in sub-Saharan Africa uses unimproved seeds, often in unfertilized, depleted fields, with yields dependent upon increasingly unreliable rainfall (see World Bank 2007).

The Multiple Dimensions of Poverty

Global poverty is about more than income, and is not automatically solved through economic growth. Poverty is characterized by early death, poor health, denial of education, and indeed the loss of childhood (Smith 2005). Thus, poverty is multidimensional and is characterized by health problems, undernutrition, child labor, illiteracy, under-five mortality, degraded environment, disempowerment, and social exclusion. Nearly 1.7 billion people live in multidimensional poverty, according to the multidimensional poverty index (MPI) constructed by the United Nations Development Programme (UNDP 2012). In sum, poverty problems are not readily solved with higher income alone.

Poverty is pervasiveness of early death. Kofi Annan said, "This [extreme poverty] is a poverty that kills" (United Nations 2005, p. 7). In some countries—Afghanistan, Chad, the Congo, Guinea-Bissau, Mali, Niger, and Sierra Leone—about one-fifth of all children die before age five from preventable causes. Life expectancy in sub-Saharan Africa is just 53. In South Asia, nearly 1 child in 12 dies before age five. The under-five mortality rate is 118 per 1,000 in low-income countries, 51 per 1,000 in middle-income countries, and 7 per 1,000 in high-income countries (World Bank 2011). Every day, an average of nearly 20,000 children in developing countries die from preventable causes. This amounted to over seven million in 2012 alone.

Poverty is hunger and poor health. The International Classification of Diseases includes "Code Z59.5—extreme poverty" (Smith 2005). About 900 million people are classified as hungry (undernourished) by the United Nations' World Food Organization (WFO). There are many other severe health deprivations. Micronutrient malnutrition affects nearly two billion; children may face lifelong disabilities (see, e.g., Alderman, Hoddinott, and Kinsey [2006]). Women with nutritional deficiencies are more likely to deliver smaller babies, who are at risk of having poor growth and development. In many poor countries, parasites are widespread. In developing countries, a woman dies during childbirth nearly every minute—very few of these women would have died if they had lived in a developed country. It has been estimated that as many as 3,000 children in Africa die from malaria each day.

Poverty is the denial of the right to a basic education. As of 2012, there were about 776 million illiterate adults in the world (UNESCO 2014). Nearly 40 percent of all adults in South Asia are illiterate. Often, students go to school only to find the teacher is absent: "teacher truancy" is a major scourge in South Asia and is also common in Africa. A child in sub-Saharan Africa and South Asia can expect to receive less than five years of schooling. In at least 12 sub-Saharan African countries, a child is more likely to die before the age of five than to attend secondary school.

Poverty is the loss of childhood. According to the International Labour Organization, there are at least 215 million child laborers (ILO 2010), and 115 million of these children are engaged in what the ILO classifies as "hazardous work." Approximately 91 million working children are under 12 years old. Millions of child laborers are trapped in slavery, trafficking, debt bondage, prostitution, pornography, and other abhorrent conditions.

Special Challenges for Poverty Reduction

It is well established that growth and development, although they are not a panacea, can reduce poverty. But the causality appears to run in both directions: it is also becoming increasingly understood that *successful poverty reduction can cause growth*. Failure to address poverty produces constraints on prospects for development, for at least four reasons:

1) Poor health, nutrition, and education lower the economic productivity of people in poverty, leading directly and indirectly to slower growth.

2) Higher income for the poor raises demand for locally produced goods (albeit of lower quality).

3) The poor often lack access to credit, which constrains growth. In particular, the result can be lost opportunities for entrepreneurship that might benefit society. It can also render the poor unable to finance their children's education, thus limiting the skilled labor force needed for development.

4) Poverty creates incentives for high fertility as a source of old-age financial security; high fertility is associated with a slower rate of economic growth (Todaro and Smith 2011, Chapter 5).

The Role of Good Governance

Good governance—which, as the editors of this volume point out in the introductory chapter, is also multidimensional—plays an essential role in achieving multidimensional poverty-reduction goals. The relationship between economic growth and effective poverty reduction is not inevitable, but it *is* possible. Economic growth helps to reduce poverty in most places, most of the time. As is well known, good governance—or at least avoidance of actively bad governance—is essential to increase growth rates and keep them high. Particularly to the extent that growth is not sufficient to reduce poverty, governance is needed to design and implement active public policies and effective, accessible basic services and social programs to attack poverty directly. Good governance plays a critical role in preventing coercion and exploitation of the poor. It provides for two-way channels of communication between the poor and both national and local government. A voice for the poor is essential to bring both longstanding and new problems—such as negative climate change impacts—to government and (more broadly) citizen attention.

Another key function of good governance is the provision of relevant and reliable information. Globally, more than two-thirds of the poor live in rural areas, and many of them are smallholder farmers using outmoded and no longer appropriate technology. Poor farmers can greatly benefit from government-provided agricultural extension information (such as has benefited farmers in the United States since the nineteenth century). Government also plays a key role in encouraging the use of improved seed varieties and other Green Revolution practices, including the expansion of irrigation. Such assistance will be all the more important as climate change becomes large enough to create conditions outside the range of farmers' experience.

Again, development itself can be constrained by a high incidence of poverty, adding to the significance of good governance in achieving more narrowly defined economic objectives, as Sisay Asefa and Wei-Chiao Huang assert in the introduction to this volume.

Why is it so difficult for the poorest of the poor to make further progress? One reason is the presence of poverty traps, which poor governance often exacerbates.

Addressing poverty traps. Poverty traps occur at both macro and micro levels. The notion of poverty traps goes back to the early days of post–World War II development economics. Nobel laureate Gunnar Myrdal called it a problem of "circular and cumulative causation" (Myrdal 1968, p. 1875). To overcome macro poverty traps, a "big push" may be needed, a concept pioneered by Paul Rosenstein-Rodan (1943), who first raised some of the basic problems that can

Governance Problems and Priorities for Local Climate Adaptation   117

underpin a poverty trap, such as lack of coordination among investors. High-fertility traps can exist because of a different kind of coordination problem: if all families had lower fertility, all would be better off, but as long as most other families are having many children, it is too economically risky for a family to be a "pioneer" in having only two children (Dasgupta 1993). Population pressures also figure in classic Malthusian traps, in which a society cannot escape from subsistence income because additional resources only go to maintain larger population sizes (Urdal 2005). Many of these concepts have been formalized in more recent years (Todaro and Smith 2011, Chapter 4). Another coordination failure is at work in the low-skills trap: workers who want skills that employers can use and employers who want equipment that workers can use may each be better off waiting for the other parties to invest first—but the result is that there are no modern jobs in a region.

Collier et al. (2003) find that countries are prone to civil war when faced with a combination of low income, slow growth, and dependence on primary commodity exports. We return to this problem, which the authors describe as part of a "conflict trap," later in the chapter.

Many of these traps can also be found at a subnational level, or even at a district scale, including low-skill traps. Others are found primarily at the micro and even individual levels.

A well-known example is the undernutrition trap, in which workers are unproductive because they have insufficient energy, and as a result they earn too little income to purchase sufficient calories and protein to improve their levels of energy (e.g., Dasgupta [1993]). This trap may not be common outside of famine conditions, but it may become a more serious concern if it interlocks with other traps to make the cycle more vicious. Similar cycles of individual deprivation can be caused by, or aggravated by, health problems that one is too poor to address, which may include mental health problems triggered or accentuated by stresses associated with living in poverty. They may also be caused by poor housing traps, in which bad housing (if not homelessness) prolongs illness, produces exposure to crime, leads to chronic sleep deprivation, and so on. Working-capital traps lead small vendors to maintain low inventories, which in turn yield low sales and result in an inability to accumulate capital to allow for a larger inventory. Microfinance has developed in part to address this problem—almost 200 million people have participated, but that leaves hundreds of millions more who might also benefit.

118 Smith

Environmental degradation can also figure into poverty traps. In common-property resource traps, overuse of resources that lack well-defined property rights or effective community management (Ostrom 2005) can lead to poverty: lakes are overfished, forests are not managed sustainably, land is overgrazed. Part of the problem is that community management of common resources has broken down. This is often a legacy of greedy colonial practices, now all too often imitated by post-colonial regimes. Once it has broken down, responsible use of shared resources is difficult to restore. Under some conditions, well-regulated privatization can be beneficial, providing an incentive to a recognized owner to monitor and maintain the value of these resources.

But in many situations, the result is merely the disenfranchisement of the poor, and the loss of their access to the natural resources on which their livelihoods have depended. In many cases, local conditions make it impossible to privatize common property efficiently, let alone equitably. Effective community management of the commons is an important priority for improved local and community governance with assistance from regional or national government levels—increasingly so as climate change threatens the productivity of these resources.

Another example is the farm erosion trap, in which the poor face such urgent need to grow more food that they have to overuse their land, even though in many cases they are aware that the result will be reduced soil fertility—hence, reduced productivity in future seasons. As a result, farmers may be trapped in a downward spiral, in which productivity gains from learning new techniques are undermined by the poorer quality of the soil. There is evidence of poverty-trap problems among farmers in Ethiopia, particularly in the impoverished region that grows enset (a type of root crop that resembles a small banana tree) (Kwak and Smith [2013]; see also Deressa [2007]).

TWO RELATED CONSTRAINTS TO ENDING POVERTY:
1) ENVIRONMENTAL DEGRADATION AND
2) POOR GOVERNANCE AND CONFLICT

Two core problems in ending global poverty (when commentators speak of "ending" global poverty they generally mean reducing it to

Governance Problems and Priorities for Local Climate Adaptation 119

"frictional" amounts, perhaps 100 to 300 million people) are 1) environmental degradation and 2) severe governance problems (including overt conflict). These dimensions of environmental and governance breakdowns are increasingly intertwined.

Conflict and Threats to Natural Resource–Based Livelihoods

Natural resource–based livelihoods are counted on in most antipoverty strategies as potential "pathways out of poverty" (World Resources Institute et al. 2005). In low-income countries, there is high dependence on natural resources: agriculture, animal husbandry, fishing, forestry, hunting, and foraging. But access to the benefits of resources is often very inequitable: in some regions, the poor have been losing control of natural-resource common areas on which they depend. Village common lands may be "spontaneously" privatized (or, to put less of a fine point on it, stolen). Many of the poor lack even basic capital, including farmland, forests, cattle, boats, and equipment. Government officials may overlook (or be paid to ignore) companies that log, fish, and mine without regard to local inhabitants or traditional rights. Governments may also designate lands as "protected," thus banning local people from earning a livelihood, while corruption remains; the result is that the poor have no incentive to take part in environmental protection. A solution to this is the principle of "pro-poor governance," which simply means empowerment of people living in poverty. Failure to provide pro-poor governance can worsen poverty, trigger conflict, or both (Todaro and Smith 2011, Section 14.5).

Consequences of Conflict

Violent conflict harms well-being in ways both obvious and unexpected, extending well beyond the immediate effects of death, injury, and destruction. People not involved in violence can be affected almost immediately, as parents lose their livelihood or become refugees and children are forced to work. Recovery from the consequences can take many years. Conflict can cause children to miss out on schooling in their most formative years, harming their well-being over the course of a lifetime (see, e.g., Barron [2010]; Blattman and Annan [2010]; Blattman and Miguel [2010]; Bundervoet, Verwimp, and Akresh [2009]; Li and Wen [2005]; Messer, Cohen, and Marchione [2001]; and Seitz [2004]).

When armed conflict first breaks out in a country or a region, more men die than women, primarily as a result of the fighting itself. But over time, more women die, as they suffer lingering consequences. Maternal mortality (dying from complications of pregnancy or childbirth) can reach about 3 percent in conflict areas such as the Democratic Republic of the Congo. The long-term effects of conflict fall most heavily on women, as these effects diminish their access to health, social welfare services, and education (Plümper and Neumayer 2006). Rape is a weapon of terror used to destroy communities and family bonds. Many victims die in rape attacks, and many more suffer long-term health consequences, including AIDS and chronic depression. Refugee children and women are at risk of rape and sexual exploitation. Refugee tent camps can spread infectious diseases such as diarrhea, measles, acute respiratory diseases, malaria, and sexually transmitted diseases, including HIV/AIDS. Refugees die of diseases at high rates—more might survive with better nourishment and rest. Evidence suggests that each additional international refugee leads to an extra 1.4 malaria cases in the host country. Meanwhile, government health spending falls, just when public health support is most needed.

Development in reverse. Violent conflict destroys capital; some that is not destroyed is diverted from productive to destructive activities (Murdoch and Sandler 2004). Additional wealth is often shipped abroad. On average, about one-tenth of a country's wealth is transferred abroad between the beginning of a conflict and its end, largely because of capital flight (Collier et al. 2003).

Countries consumed by conflict have an estimated average annual growth of −3.3 percent, constituting what is known as "development in reverse." Incomes following a civil war average 15 percent lower than before the war. This translates to approximately 30 percent more people living in extreme poverty. The loss of human capital is substantial: when children lose out on their education, it has permanent effects in many cases, even though some students later return to school. Spending on education falls during conflicts, severely exacerbating the problems. The torn social fabric is, in itself, destructive to development opportunities.

Theories of the causes of conflict vary, including the presence of horizontal inequalities (Stewart 2000, 2008), severe scarcity of basic resources, as in some interpretations of the Darfur conflicts (UNEP 2007), commitment problems between government and (potential) rebels (Powell 2006), and the struggle to control valuable natural resources for export (Collier 2007).

Climate Stressors as a Trigger for Conflict

Evidence is emerging that climate stressors are also important triggers for conflict. In particular, although climate change may be neither a necessary nor a sufficient cause for conflict, climate can be a contributing and triggering stressor, acting in concert with other political, social, or economic variables. This is of growing concern, given the range of dire consequences for Africa and some other regions of the developing world predicted under most climate-change scenarios (Cline 2007; Intergovernmental Panel on Climate Change 2007; NOAA 2010; Parry et al. 2007; World Bank 2010a), including prolonged droughts, expanded desertification, increased severity of storms, higher temperatures and more severe heat waves, deteriorated water resources, and reduced crop yields.

Climate change may endanger livelihoods, intensify conflicts over resources, and induce greater migration within, and across, national boundaries. In countries with weak governments and institutions, these added stresses may lead to greater instability. Countries with greater societal resilience are likely to withstand these stresses better, as well as to build greater resilience to climate change. Moreover, a growing literature documents a link between rainfall levels and violence, as well as between high temperatures and violence or civil conflict (Burke et al. 2009; Miguel 2013).

Adaptation Responses and Their Impacts on Conflict Risk

Most discussion about climate change has been focused on approaches to reducing greenhouse gas emissions. But most low-income countries emit relatively small amounts of greenhouse gases (although the burning involved in deforestation and the resulting decrease in carbon dioxide absorption are significant contributors). And for low-income developing countries, climate change impacts are already arriving and must be responded to. Thus, the central focus in these countries is on adaptation to current and anticipated adverse climate change (see, e.g., Adger et al. [2007]; Dinar et al. [2008]; Malik and Smith [2012]; Mendelsohn [2012]; World Bank [2010b]; and World Resources Institute et al. [2011]).

There are two basic approaches to adaptation. Planned (or policy-driven) adaptation is undertaken by governments. In contrast, autonomous adaptation is undertaken by individuals, families, and communities; Malik and Smith (2012) give some key examples, including altering crop or livestock varieties, changing livelihoods, increasing exploitation of common pool resources, moving locally (such as to higher ground), and migrating temporarily or permanently, either within a country or internationally. Almost certainly, autonomous adaptation will be the predominant form of adaptation. Good governance acts as a complement for autonomous adaptation (and, at least, avoids thwarting beneficial responses). But governments have little experience with this role, and in some cases their incentives may lie in implementing policies that have the effect of undermining otherwise constructive adaptation measures in poor communities, such as removing control of natural resources from communities and placing it in the hands of officials who mismanage or misuse that control.

PERSPECTIVES ON GOOD GOVERNANCE FOR ADAPTATION

General Considerations

Policy effectiveness, economic efficiency, and equity may be improved to the extent that seven conditions are in place. Policymakers want to ensure that

1) a flexible, well-designed approach to interaction is implemented between adaptation policy and the autonomous adaptation setting;

2) they gain an improved understanding of how agents adapt in the absence of planned adaptation, and how adaptation is likely to change in response to planned adaption policies;

3) the moral hazard of agents in response to planned adaptation is addressed;

4) those autonomously adapting have a voice in adaptation policies that affect them;

5) planned adaptation does not reduce opportunity for autonomous adaptation, and that planned adaptation accounts for indirect impacts (for example, the diversion of water resources from areas with traditional rights to cities or irrigated districts with political clout, and an accounting for the impacts of government restrictions on development in low-lying areas);

6) negative externalities of autonomous adaptation are addressed effectively—e.g., lowered water tables, salination, and worsened sanitation in neighboring areas; and

7) positive externalities of autonomous adaptation, such as learning across neighboring communities, are effectively encouraged and augmented.

Climate Change Adaptation through Migration

Threats to natural resource–based livelihoods are expected to increase the rate of rural-to-urban migration (see, e.g., Hatton and Williamson [2003]; Marchiori, Maystadt, and Schumacher 2011; McLeman and Smit [2006]; Naudé [2010]; and Warner et al. [2009]). Lower productivity increases the wedge (or gap) separating urban and rural incomes, spurring migration that may eventually include hundreds of millions of people. Migration on such a scale would result in competition for resources and employment that would heighten the potential for conflict and instability. A case in point is reported from Bangladesh, where economic competition between "climate migrants" and residents of destination areas has led in some cases to violence. Among the causes of tension between the two groups was a drop in wages—especially wages in the informal sector—that was due to the influx of migrants. In another case in point, this one from Sudan, environmental and farming changes led to changed seasonal migration routes, worsening tensions among pastoralists (those who raise and herd livestock) and between pastoralists and farmers.

Governance challenges of heightened competition for resources. The absence of established institutions for managing natural resources in areas newly settled by different ethnic groups has led to environmental degradation; in turn, the resulting degradation has exacerbated resource scarcity, fueled tensions, and led to violent conflict (see, e.g., Barnett and Adger [2007]; Bronkhorst [2011]; Hsiang, Meng, and Cane [2011]; Sayne [2011]; Stark, Mataya, and Lubovich [2009]; Theisen [2008]; and UNEP [2007]). Conflict is more likely to emerge in the absence of a well-defined or well-enforced system of property rights: traditional inhabitants of an area may stake customary claims to land that formally may be (has been declared to be) open-access public land. Good-quality formal governance must at least take traditional governance into account in planning and policy. As a case in point from Nigeria, feed and water shortages caused partly by drought and desertification induced pastoralists to move south, outside their traditional seasonal grazing patterns. In turn, sedentary farmers responded to weather-related changes by cultivating more land. This left pastoralists with little uncontested land on which to graze and water their animals, leading to violent conflicts between identity groups finding themselves in contested territory, such as farmers and herdsmen (pastoralists). As a second case in point, in Kenya, increased drought induced pastoralists to adopt more sedentary livelihoods, settling near water sources that farmers also relied upon and that were already at risk.

A related challenge is that in the process of both autonomous and planned adaptation to climate change, traditional access to natural resources can be restricted, and the result can heighten tensions. Without effective formal or traditional institutions to deal with these consequences, autonomous adaptation can increase the risk of conflict. A case in point comes from coastal Bangladesh, where water from tube wells became more prone to saltwater contamination, which in turn induced inhabitants of affected areas to draw water from unaffected wells in neighboring areas. This, of course, fueled tensions—and led to episodes of violent conflict—with the inhabitants of these areas.

Planned adaptation, government policies, and conflict. Planned adaptation (and, more generally, government policy) can increase the risk of conflict when it acts to restrict feasible autonomous adaptation (Malik and Smith 2012). For example, policies to vacate densely populated areas that have become subject to inundation increase pressures on adjacent land; this can clearly give rise to conflict. In contrast, constructing barriers such as floodgates to protect vulnerable land might, in some circumstances, avoid conflict risk. But building such barriers may also have unintended consequences, such as harming the livelihoods of others by eroding coastlines and reducing fishing opportunities along adjoining areas of the coast.

To cite another example, policies restricting migration within or across countries could avoid tensions and reduce the risk of conflict. But restrictions could also increase the risk because migration is a safety valve that itself represents an important form of autonomous adaptation.

Government influence in preventing communal conflicts depends on two key factors.

First, it depends on whether government is strong enough to protect people and communities from external threats—i.e., strong enough to enforce property rights and impose needed regulations on communities. If government is weak, property rights cannot be protected, and effective planned adaptation is infeasible; hence, the possibility of conflict between the two communities cannot be avoided.

Second, while government must have sufficient authority and strength to enforce the peace, the poor may be subjected to equal or greater harm when government is unduly coercive, biased, or unwilling to decentralize authority. The quality of governance relationships between the central government and local communities (or regions) is of critical importance. At one extreme, government repression may trigger conflict. However, if national or regional government neglects a community, this may also trigger conflict when the community perceives the government to be ineffective, if not hostile. Poor governance responses to climate change can hinder autonomous adaptation rather than complement it, also resulting in conflict. The situation can be aggravated if government is seen as siding with one community over another. For example, conflict may result if government prevents migration from a severely climate-affected community to an area less affected that may be perceived as unfairly privileged. International peer review of governments can play an important role in improving individual country governance practices; a good example is the New Partnership for Africa's Development (NEPAD), an activity of the African Union (see http://www.nepad.org/).

126 Smith

In these ways, good governance plays a central role in poverty reduction in general, and particularly in response to looming development problems caused by climate change. By anticipating and constructively responding to these problems, good governance can lessen the harmful effects of climate change on a government's people.

Note

This chapter is based on a Sichel Lecture of a similar title in the series on the Political Economy of Good Governance, which was delivered on the campus of Western Michigan University on April 10, 2013. The presentation drew on joint work with Arun Malik, with input from Elizabeth Chacko, Marie Price, and Jonathan Rothbaum; these contributions greatly benefited the preparation of this chapter. I would also like to thank participants of the Sichel Lecture for excellent discussions, particularly Sisay Asefa and Wei-Chiao Huang. Research assistance from the Institute for International Economic Policy at George Washington University is gratefully acknowledged. Any errors are my own.

References

Adger, W. Neil, Shardul Agrawala, M. Monirul Qader Mirza, Cecilia Conde, Karen O'Brien, Juan Pulhin, Roger Pulwarty, Barry Smit, and Kiyoshi Takahashi. 2007. "Assessment of Adaptation Practices, Options, Constraints, and Capacity." In *Climate Change 2007: Impacts, Adaptation, and Vulnerability. Contribution of Working Group II to the Fourth Assessment Report of the Intergovernmental Panel on Climate Change*, Martin Parry, Osvaldo Canziani, Jean Palutikof, Paul van der Linden, and Clair Hanson, eds. Cambridge: Cambridge University Press, pp. 717–743.

Alderman, Harold, John Hoddinott, and Bill Kinsey. 2006. "Long Term Consequences of Early Childhood Malnutrition." *Oxford Economic Papers* 58(3): 450–474.

Barnett, Jon, and W. Neil Adger. 2007. "Climate Change, Human Security, and Violent Conflict." *Political Geography* 26(6): 639–655.

Barron, Patrick. 2010. "CDD in Post-Conflict and Conflict-Affected Areas: Experiences from East Asia." World Development Report 2011 background paper. Washington, DC: World Bank. http://web.worldbank.org/archive/website01306/web/pdf/wdr%20background%20paper_barron_0.pdf (accessed November 12, 2014).

Blattman, Christopher, and Jeannie Annan. 2010. "The Consequences of Child Soldiering." *Review of Economics and Statistics* 92(4): 882–898.

Blattman, Christopher, and Edward Miguel. 2010. "Civil War." *Journal of Economic Literature* 48(1): 3–57.

Bronkhorst, Salomé. 2011. *Climate Change and Conflict: Lessons for Conflict Resolution from the Southern Sahel of Sudan*. Report prepared by the African Centre for the Constructive Resolution of Disputes (ACCORD). Mount Edgecombe, South Africa: ACCORD.

Bundervoet, Tom, Philip Verwimp, and Richard Akresh. 2009. "Health and Civil War in Rural Burundi." *Journal of Human Resources* 44(2): 536–563.

Burke, Marshall B., Edward Miguel, Shanker Satyanath, John A. Dykema, and David B. Lobell. 2009. "Warming Increases the Risk of Civil War in Africa." *Proceedings of the National Academy of Sciences* 106(49): 20670–20674.

Cline, William R. 2007. *Global Warming and Agriculture: Impact Estimates by Country*. Washington, DC: Center for Global Development and Peterson Institute for International Economics.

Collier, Paul. 2007. *The Bottom Billion: Why the Poorest Countries Are Failing and What Can Be Done about It.* New York: Oxford University Press.

Collier, Paul, V. L. Elliott, Håvard Hegre, Anke Hoeffler, Marta Reynal-Querol, and Nicholas Sambanis. 2003. *Breaking the Conflict Trap: Civil War and Development Policy*. A World Bank Policy Research Report. Washington, DC: World Bank; and Oxford: Oxford University Press. http://www-wds.worldbank.org/external/default/WDSContentServer/IW3P/IB/2003/06/30/000094946_0306190405396/Rendered/PDF/multi0page.pdf (accessed November 13, 2014).

Dasgupta, Partha. 1993. *An Inquiry into Well-Being and Destitution*. New York: Clarendon Press.

Deressa, Temesgen Tadesse. 2007. "Measuring the Economic Impact of Climate Change on Ethiopian Agriculture: Ricardian Approach." World Bank Policy Research Working Paper No. 4342. Washington, DC: World Bank.

Dinar, Ariel, Rashid Hassan, Robert Mendelsohn, and James Benhin. 2008. *Climate Change and Agriculture in Africa: Impact Assessment and Adaptation Strategies*. Earthscan Climate Series. London: Taylor and Francis Group/Earthscan.

Hatton, Timothy J., and Jeffrey G. Williamson. 2003. "Demographic and Economic Pressure on Emigration Out of Africa." *Scandinavian Journal of Economics* 105(3): 465–486.

Hsiang, Solomon M., Kyle C. Meng, and Mark A. Cane. 2011. "Civil Conflicts Are Associated with the Global Climate." *Nature* 476(7361): 438–441.

Intergovernmental Panel on Climate Change. 2007. *Climate Change 2007: Synthesis Report. Summary for Policymakers*. Cambridge: Cambridge University Press.

International Labour Organization (ILO). 2010. *Facts on Child Labour 2010*. Geneva: International Labour Office.

Kwak, Sungil, and Stephen C. Smith. 2013. "Regional Agricultural Endowments and Shifts of Poverty Trap Equilibria: Evidence from Ethiopian Panel Data." *Journal of Development Studies* 49(7): 955–975.

Li, Quan, and Ming Wen. 2005. "The Immediate and Lingering Effects of Armed Conflict on Adult Mortality: A Time-Series Cross-National Analysis." *Journal of Peace Research* 42(4): 471–492.

Malik, Arun S., and Stephen C. Smith. 2012. "Adaptation to Climate Change in Low-Income Countries: Lessons from Current Research and Needs from Future Research." *Climate Change Economics* 3(2): 1–22.

Marchiori, Luca, Jean-François Maystadt, and Ingmar Schumacher. 2011. "The Impact of Climate Variations on Migration in Sub-Saharan Africa." Paper presented at the Conference on the Economics of Adaptation to Climate Change in Low-Income Countries, held in Washington, DC, May 18–19.

McLeman, Robert, and Barry Smit. 2006. "Migration as an Adaptation to Climate Change." *Climatic Change* 76(1–2): 31–53.

Mendelsohn, Robert. 2012. "The Economics of Adaptation to Climate Change in Developing Countries." *Climate Change Economics* 3(2): 1–21. http://www.worldscientific.com/doi/abs/10.1142/S2010007812500066?queryID=%24%7BresultBean.queryID%7D (accessed February 5, 2015).

Messer, Ellen, Marc J. Cohen, and Thomas Marchione. 2001. "Conflict: A Cause and Effect of Hunger." In *Environmental Change and Security Project, Seventh Annual Report*, Geoffrey D. Dabelko, ed. Washington, DC: Woodrow Wilson Center, Environmental Change and Security Project, pp. 1–20.

Miguel, Edward. 2013. "Conflict, Climate, and Economic Development in Africa." Keynote address presented at the Centre for the Study of African Economies' annual conference, held in Oxford, March 17–19.

Murdoch, James C., and Todd Sandler. 2004. "Civil Wars and Economic Growth: Spatial Dispersion." *American Journal of Political Science* 48(1): 138–151.

Myrdal, Gunnar. 1968. *Asian Drama*. New York: Pantheon.

National Oceanic and Atmospheric Administration (NOAA). 2010. *NOAA: Past Decade Warmest on Record According to Scientists in 48 Countries*. Washington, DC: National Oceanic and Atmospheric Administration. http://www.noaanews.noaa.gov/stories2010/20100728_stateoftheclimate.html (accessed January 19, 2015).

Naudé, Wim. 2010. "The Determinants of Migration from Sub-Saharan African Countries." *Journal of African Economies* 19(3): 330–356.

North, Douglass C. 1990. *Institutions, Institutional Change, and Economic Performance*. Cambridge and New York: Cambridge University Press.

Ostrom, Elinor. 2005. *Understanding Institutional Diversity*. Princeton, NJ: Princeton University Press.

Parry, M. L., O. F. Canziani, J. P. Palutikof, P. J. van der Linden, and C. E. Hanson, eds. 2007. *Contribution of Working Group II to the Fourth Assessment Report of the Intergovernmental Panel on Climate Change*. Cambridge: Cambridge University Press.

Plümper, Thomas, and Eric Neumayer. 2006. "The Unequal Burden of War: The Effect of Armed Conflict on the Gender Gap in Life Expectancy." *International Organization* 60(3): 723–754.

Powell, Robert. 2006. "War as a Commitment Problem." *International Organization* 60(1): 169–203.

Rosenstein-Rodan, Paul N. 1943. "Problems of Industrialisation of Eastern and South-Eastern Europe." *Economic Journal* 53(210–211): 202–211.

Sab, Randa, and Stephen C. Smith. 2002. "Human Capital Convergence: A Joint Estimation Approach." *IMF Staff Papers* 49(2): 200–211.

Sayne, Aaron. 2011. "Climate Change Adaptation and Conflict in Nigeria." USIP Special Report No. 274. Washington, DC: United States Institute of Peace.

Seitz, Klaus. 2004. *Education and Conflict: The Role of Education in the Creation, Prevention, and Resolution of Societal Crises—Consequences for Development Cooperation*. Berlin: German Technical Cooperation.

Smith, Stephen C. 2005. *Ending Global Poverty: A Guide to What Works*. New York: Palgrave Macmillan.

Stark, Jeffrey, Christine Mataya, and Kelley Lubovich. 2009. "Climate Change, Adaptation, and Conflict: A Preliminary Review of the Issues." CMM Discussion Paper No. 1. Prepared for the Office of Conflict Management and Mitigation, USAID. Washington, DC: United States Agency for International Development.

Stewart, Frances. 2000. "The Root Causes of Humanitarian Emergencies." In *War, Hunger, and Displacement: The Origins of Humanitarian Emergencies*. Vol. 1, *Analysis,* E. Wayne Nafziger, Frances Stewart, and Raimo Väyrynen, eds. Oxford: Oxford University Press, pp. 1–42.

————, ed. 2008. *Horizontal Inequalities and Conflict: Understanding Group Violence in Multiethnic Societies*. New York: Palgrave Macmillan.

Theisen, Ole Magnus. 2008. "Blood and Soil? Resource Scarcity and Internal Armed Conflict Revisited." *Journal of Peace Research* 45(6): 801–818.

Todaro, Michael P., and Stephen C. Smith. 2011. *Economic Development*. 11th ed. Reading, MA: Addison-Wesley.

United Nations. 2005. *In Larger Freedom: Towards Development, Security, and Human Rights for All*. Report of the Secretary-General. New York: United Nations.

———. 2012. *The Millennium Development Goals Report 2012*. New York: United Nations. http://www.un.org/millenniumgoals/pdf/MDG%20 Report%202012.pdf (accessed January 19, 2015).

United Nations Development Programme (UNDP). 2012. *Human Development Report 2012*. New York: United Nations Development Programme.

United Nations Educational, Scientific, and Cultural Organization (UNESCO). 2014. *Database*. Paris: UNESCO. http://www.unesco.org/new/en/unesco/ resources/publications/unesdoc-database/ (accessed January 19, 2015).

United Nations Environment Programme (UNEP). 2007. *Sudan: Post-Conflict Environmental Assessment*. Nairobi, Kenya: United Nations Environment Programme. http://postconflict.unep.ch/publications/UNEP_Sudan.pdf (accessed February 5, 2015).

Urdal, Henrik. 2005. "People vs. Malthus: Population Pressure, Environmental Degradation, and Armed Conflict Revisited." *Journal of Peace Research* 42(2005): 417–434.

Warner, Koko, Charles Ehrhart, Alex de Sherbinin, Susana Adamo, and Tricia Chai-Onn. 2009. *In Search of Shelter: Mapping the Effects of Climate Change on Human Migration and Displacement*. New York: United Nations University, CARE International, and CIESIN–Columbia University.

World Bank. 2007. *World Development Report 2008: Agriculture for Development*. Washington, DC: World Bank.

———. 2010a. *Development and Climate Change, World Development Report 2010*. Washington, DC: World Bank.

———. 2010b. *The Economics of Adaptation to Climate Change*. A Synthesis Report. Washington, DC: World Bank.

———. 2011. *World Development Report 2011: Conflict, Security, and Development*. Washington, DC: World Bank.

———. 2013. *State of the Poor: Where Are the Poor and Where Are They Poorest?* Washington, DC: World Bank. http://www.worldbank.org/content/ dam/Worldbank/document/State_of_the_poor_paper_April17.pdf (accessed September 23, 2014).

World Resources Institute, United Nations Development Programme, United Nations Environment Programme, and World Bank. 2005. *The Wealth of the Poor: Managing Ecosystems to Fight Poverty*. World Resources Report 2005. Washington, DC: World Resources Institute.

———. 2011. *Decision Making in a Changing Climate—Adaptation Challenges and Choices*. World Resources Report 2010–2011. Washington, DC: World Resources Institute.

7

The Challenges of Good Governance and Leadership in Developing Countries

Cases from Africa and China

Sisay Asefa
Wei-Chiao Huang
Western Michigan University

UNDERSTANDING AND MEASURING GOOD GOVERNANCE FOR SUSTAINABLE HUMAN DEVELOPMENT

The World Governance Indicators (WGI) project, which can be found at www.govindicators.org, defines "governance" as consisting of "the traditions and institutions by which authority in a country is exercised" (World Bank 2014, p. 1). This includes how governments are selected, monitored, and replaced, including their capacity to formulate and implement sound policies, provide public services, and earn the respect of citizens and institutions that determine economic and social interactions (Kaufmann 2010). WGI identifies the following six core governance components: 1) voice and accountability, 2) political stability and the absence of violence, 3) government effectiveness, 4) regulatory quality, 5) rule of law, and 6) control of corruption.

Based on these measures, Nordic states in Europe such as Sweden, Denmark, and Norway have a high standard of governance.

Good governance is rare in Africa, but it exists in a few countries such as Botswana, Mauritius, Senegal, and Ghana. From a development perspective, good governance is a major means for promoting sustainable development, reducing poverty, and maintaining peace. Countries with good governance are efficient in delivery of public services, follow

131

the rule of law, and have inclusive institutions responsive to the needs of citizens. They are transparent and promote participation as well as show respect for citizens and allow for a free press and for overall freedom of expression. Some typical characteristics of good governance are listed in the diagram shown in Figure 7.1. Autocratic and dysfunctional governments are unable to meet all or some of these commitments.

Good governance also reduces poverty, which can be measured in at least two ways. The income approach is simply based on the number of people below global poverty standards, defined as $1.25 a day in U.S. dollars. Another, more comprehensive recent innovation in measuring poverty is the Multidimensional Poverty Index (MPI), which disaggregates three components of human development: 1) health, 2) education, and 3) standard of living, as described below:

- Health (measured by two indicators with equal one-sixth weight on the MPI scale): whether any child has died in the household, and whether any adult or child in the family is malnourished.
- Education (measured by two indicators with equal one-sixth weight on the MPI scale): whether no household member completed five years of schooling, and whether any school-aged child is out of school for grades one through eight.

Figure 7.1 A Simple Model of Good Governance

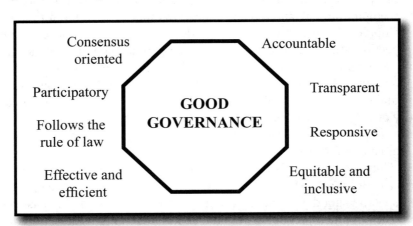

SOURCE: Based on Collier (2007).

The Challenges of Good Governance in Developing Countries   133

- Standard of Living (measured by six indicators with equal one-eighteenth weight on the MPI scale): These deprivations include the lack of electricity; insufficiently safe drinking water; inadequate sanitation; inadequate flooring; unimproved cooking fuel; and the lack of more than one of the following assets—telephone, radio, TV, bicycle, and motorbike.

Table 7.1 compares MPI and income poverty for select countries, including the African nations of Ethiopia, Angola, the Congo, Ghana, Kenya, Niger, Tanzania, and Zimbabwe, along with other developing countries in Asia and Latin America. By MPI ranking, Ethiopia's score of 103 is at the bottom, just above Niger's 104, with 90 percent of its population considered to be multidimensionally poor.

GOVERNANCE, DEVELOPMENT, AND MULTIDIMENSIONAL POVERTY INDEX (MPI) RELATIONSHIPS

Governance, human development, and MPI indicators are linked. Poor governance leads to low MPI; low Human Development Index (HDI), which measures achievement in terms of having a long and healthy life, being knowledgeable, and having a decent standard of living; and high corruption, as measured by the Corruption Perceptions Index (CPI). The following table shows the level and relationships of human development, governance, and the Ibrahim Index of African Governance (IIAG), along with two measures of poverty—1) income and 2) MPI. The measurement ranges are as follows: HDI: 0–1 (0 being the lowest); IIAG: 1–100 (1 being the lowest, 100 the best); and CPI: 10–1 (10 being the lowest, 1 the best) (Table 7.2).

For the African countries listed, Botswana has the best governance ranking (No. 3 by the IIAG measure), while Somalia has the worst governance, with a rank of 52. Using MPI, Ethiopia is multidimensionally the poorest. The HDI for Ethiopia is just above that of Eritrea, 0.36 to 0.35. This means that claims of rapid growth in Ethiopia have not translated into human development and poverty reduction.

IIAG is a comprehensive measure of governance focused on African states based on 57 variables categorized into five indices that include 1) safety and human security; 2) rule of law, transparency, and corrup-

Table 7.1 Comparative Income Poverty and Multidimensional Poverty Measures

Country	Year	MPI value	MPI rank	Multidimensional poverty H_M (proportion of poor)	A (average intensity of deprivations)	Income poverty $1.25 a day (proportion of poor) Value	Rank	$2 a day (proportion of poor) Value	Rank
Kazakhstan	2006	0.002	7	0.006	0.369	0.031	23	0.172	29
Thailand	2005	0.006	16	0.016	0.385	0.020	1	0.115	20
Ecuador	2003	0.009	24	0.022	0.416	0.047	26	0.128	23
Mexico	2006	0.015	29	0.040	0.389	0.020	1	0.048	16
Brazil	2003	0.039	39	0.085	0.460	0.052	29	0.127	21
Colombia	2005	0.041	40	0.092	0.441	0.160	42	0.279	35
Dominican Republic	2000	0.048	42	0.111	0.433	0.050	28	0.151	27
China	2003	0.056	44	0.125	0.449	0.159	41	0.363	41
Vietnam	2002	0.075	50	0.143	0.525	0.215	50	0.484	51
Indonesia	2007	0.095	53	0.208	0.459	0.075	31	0.490	52
Ghana	2008	0.140	57	0.301	0.464	0.300	57	0.536	56
Zimbabwe	2006	0.174	60	0.385	0.452				
Bolivia	2003	0.175	61	0.363	0.483	0.196	46	0.303	38
Nicaragua	2001	0.211	64	0.407	0.519	0.158	40	0.318	40
Laos	2006	0.267	68	0.472	0.565	0.440	46	0.768	73
Pakistan	2007	0.275	70	0.510	0.540	0.226	53	0.603	59
Yemen	2006	0.283	71	0.525	0.539	0.175	43	0.466	49
Bangladesh	2007	0.291	73	0.578	0.504	0.496	71	0.813	80

India	2005	0.296	74	0.554	0.535	0.416	64	0.756	70
Kenya	2003	0.302	76	0.604	0.500	0.197	47	0.399	43
Haiti	2006	0.306	77	0.573	0.533	0.549	76	0.721	67
Côte d'Ivoire	2005	0.320	78	0.522	0.614	0.233	55	0.468	50
Nepal	2006	0.350	82	0.647	0.540	0.551	77	0.776	76
Tanzania	2008	0.367	84	0.653	0.563	0.885	93	0.966	93
D.R. Congo	2007	0.393	88	0.732	0.537	0.592	79	0.795	77
Madagascar	2004	0.413	91	0.705	0.585	0.678	86	0.896	87
Angola	2001	0.452	93	0.774	0.584	0.543	89	0.900	88
Ethiopia	2005	0.582	103	0.900	0.647	0.390	62	0.775	75
Niger	2006	0.642	104	0.927	0.693	0.659	85	0.856	85

NOTE: "MPI" = Multidimensional Poverty Index.
SOURCE: World Bank (2014).

136 Asefa and Huang

Table 7.2 Comparative Measures of Governance and Poverty for Selected African States

Country	HDI	CPI	IIAG (%)	Income poverty (MPI) (%)
Ethiopia	0.36	2.7	33 (47)	40 (89)
Eritrea	0.35	2.5	49 (33)	—
Sudan	0.41	1.6	48 (33)	—
Somalia	—	1.0	52 (7)	—
Djibouti	0.43	3.0	49 (49)	19 (29)
Ghana	0.54	3.9	7 (15)	30 (31)
Kenya	0.51	2.2	24 (53)	20 (49)
Botswana	0.63	6.1	3 (78)	30 (—)
Tanzania	0.47	3.0	58 (59)	33 (65)
Nigeria	0.46	2.4	43 (42)	55 (55)
Uganda	0.44	2.4	55 (19)	29 (72)

NOTE: "HDI" stands for "Human Development Index." "CPI" stands for "Corruption Perceptions Index." "IIAG" stands for "Ibrahim Index of African Governance." "MPI" stands for "Multidimensional Poverty Index." — = data not available.
SOURCE: World Bank (2014).

tion; 3) sustainable economic development; 4) participation and human rights; and 5) human development (education, health, and income). Table 7.3 provides a ranking of scores that are assigned grades based on groups of countries in terms of quality of governance in percentages (ranging from 10 to 100).

THE ROLE OF GOOD GOVERNANCE IN SUSTAINABLE DEVELOPMENT AND POVERTY REDUCTION

Good governance plays an essential role in achieving multidimensional poverty-reduction goals. Economic growth helps to reduce poverty only in good governance states in most cases. Rapid and narrow growth driven by foreign aid can create misery and repression under autocratic governance. Promoting rapid growth cannot reduce poverty unless there is good governance present to design and implement inclusive development policies and social programs to attack poverty directly. Economic development involves economic growth plus struc-

The Challenges of Good Governance in Developing Countries   137

Table 7.3 2006 Ibrahim Index of African Governance (IIAG) Scores for African States

Scores: 100–66	Scores: 65–58	Scores: 57–51	Scores: 50–47	Scores: 46–18
Good: grade A	Above average: grade B	Average: grade C	Poor: grade D	Failed/rogue: grade F
Mauritius 85.1	Malawi 63.9	Mozambique 57.1	Ethiopia 50.9	Eritrea 46.5
Seychelles 79.8	Lesotho 63.3	Mali 55.9	Mauritania 50.8	Gabon 45.6
Cape Verde 74.7	Benin 62.5	Niger 55.5	Zimbabwe 50.4	Central African Rep. 43.6
Botswana 74.1	Comoros 61.9	Cameroon 55.4	Swaziland 50.2	Angola 43.3
South Africa 71.5	Tanzania 61.6	Djibouti 55.2	Burundi 50.0	Sudan 34.2
Namibia 70.9	Madagascar 60.4	Gambia 55.2	Equatorial Guinea 49.2	Chad 33.9
Ghana 70.1	Kenya 59.1	Congo 53.3	Sierra Leone 49.1	Congo 29.8
Gabon 69.4	Rwanda 59.1	Togo 53.0	Liberia 48.7	Somalia 18.9
São Tomé and Principé 68.3	Uganda 58.3	Guinea-Bissau 51.9	Nigeria 48.5	
Senegal 66.1	Burkina Faso 58.3		Guinea 47.8	
	Zambia 58.3			

SOURCE: Rotberg and Gisselquist (2007).

tural change toward diversification and a broader participation of citizens in the growth process, including integrated market development. Taking steps away from permanent dependence on subsistence agriculture requires good governance policies such as land reform that secures land ownership for citizens and farmers as well as providing necessary extension services such as farmer education, credit, and improved farming inputs. Positive economic transformation is impossible until a transformation occurs in which political leaders and citizens support socioeconomic and political transformation by cooperation.

ADDRESSING POVERTY TRAPS AND DEVELOPMENT COORDINATION FAILURE WITH GOOD GOVERNANCE

A cross-cutting primary reason for the persistence of poverty and food insecurity traps in Ethiopia and Africa is poor governance at both the macro and micro levels. The idea of poverty traps goes back to post-war development economics. Swedish Nobel laureate Gunnar Myrdal (1968) called it a problem of "circular and cumulative causation." A country can find itself in a high fertility trap with rapid population growth that adds to problems of poverty. Population pressures lead to a Malthusian trap, in which a society cannot escape from a subsistence economy because of lack of additional resources necessary to maintain larger population sizes. For example, Ethiopia is the second-largest populated country in Africa; it has more than 90 million people and is growing at an annual rate of 3 percent (Todaro and Smith 2014, p. 4), yet it has a very low ranking on poverty scales. Low-quality expansion of education at all levels creates a low-skills trap that prevents employers from finding skilled workers. Good governance promotes employment by focusing on high-quality education and by creating effective partnerships between employers and universities and colleges through programs such as training internships. Furthermore, requiring better pay for lecturers and teachers helps to retain high-quality teachers, which can transform the quality of education at all levels.

POOR GOVERNANCE AS THE DRIVER OF CONFLICT AND POVERTY TRAPS

The conflict trap, analyzed by Collier (2007), shows how certain economic conditions make a country prone to civil war and to the ensuing cycle of violence, from which it is difficult to escape. His study found that countries are prone to civil war when faced with a combination of low income, dependence on primary commodity exports, and poor governance that is not inclusive, along with high income inequality. A study conducted by the Oslo Peace Research Institute projected peace and conflict patterns globally until 2050. The estimates show a decrease in worldwide violence in general, except in a few countries, which include African states such as Ethiopia and Nigeria. Ethiopia is considered vulnerable on the basis of security, ideological, socioeconomic, religious and ethnic conflicts and how the state responds to these conflicts. Good governance in Africa and Ethiopia can proactively prevent future conflicts and wars. Nigeria suffers from religious-based

The Challenges of Good Governance in Developing Countries 139

extremism waged through violent acts perpetrated by a group called Boko Haram. Its edicts call for no western education for Nigerians, especially women, and the group wants to turn Nigeria, by far the largest country of Africa with a population of 170 million, into an Islamic state. Recently Boko Haram captured 250 girls from a school to sell as modern slaves. Nigeria is rich in petroleum and other natural resources and just surpassed South Africa in terms of gross national product (GNP), but it is one of the most corrupt African states; it cannot even protect its citizens from this violent extremist group, and its survival as a state is in doubt (Gates 2014).

Another development trap is the hunger and health trap, where workers are unproductive because they have insufficient energy, and they earn too little income to purchase sufficient calories and protein to improve their levels of energy and productivity. These traps also lead to hunger and famine, which become more severe if they interlock with other traps to make the cycle more vicious. Cycles of human deprivation can be caused by health problems that the poor cannot address, including mental health problems triggered by stresses associated with living in absolute poverty, hunger, and inadequate housing, which causes exposure to crime. Lack of working capital and credit access traps small business vendors and farmers. This is also a major problem, given that 70 percent of Africans make their living in agriculture. In states such as Ethiopia, the percentage can reach as high as 85. This leads to low sales and income and an inability to acquire financial capital and credit because of the lack of effective microfinancing necessary to address this problem. Still other forms of traps can be caused by community or citizen powerlessness, driven by repressive and autocratic governance (Todaro and Smith 2014).

Environmental and natural resource depletion, including soil and land degradation, also contribute to poverty and conflict traps. In the case of common property resources, overuse of resources because of a lack of secured ownership of property and land rights for farmers and a lack of effective community management of common resources can produce poverty and conflict (Ostrom 1990). Lakes and rivers may be overfished, forests may be destroyed, and pasture land overgrazed. Traditional community management of common resources can break down if foreign private investors are driven by or aligned with dictatorial regimes. The land or soil erosion and deforestation trap is one that the poor encounter because of an urgent need to grow more food, and it may lead to overuse of the land or the soil, even though they are aware that the result will be reduced soil fertility, hence a decrease in productivity in future seasons. Thus, farmers may be trapped into a cycle of low productivity, which is exacerbated by the lack of appropriate sustainable technology. This results in a practice called "soil mining," in which they have no choice but to deplete that resource.

Government support for improved technology and research could ameliorate this dilemma. For example, there is evidence of a poverty trap among farmers in Ethiopia, particularly in the banana-growing region and the densely populated highlands, and to a lesser extent even in the pastoral communities of the lowlands. It is vital that research continue to uncover a pattern of natural land degradation and deforestation that has taken place since the widespread confiscation of land in 1975 by a military junta.

LACK OF GOOD GOVERNANCE AS A DRIVER OF CORRUPTION TRAPS

Promoting good governance that is accountable, transparent, honest, and participatory, that guarantees economic freedom—i.e., the right of citizens to freely exchange goods and contract with each other in business—and that is based on secured property rights, including land rights, is crucial for the progress of Ethiopia and for all of Africa. This is only possible by moving forward with constitutional reforms that place limits on government officials to prevent the abuse of power, guarantee economic freedoms, and control the negative incentives that drive corruption. A clear legal delineation and separation of public political activities from private economic activities is necessary to reduce corruption.

Corruption can be defined as postconstitutional opportunism aimed at getting benefits for individuals or a group at the expense of society. Once a constitution is adopted, there is an incentive on the part of groups to benefit through capture of the state's redistributive power. One form of corruption, called "rent seeking," occurs when individuals and groups expend resources to negatively affect the distributional outcome. Effective control of corruption must be based on institutional and constitutional reforms to constrain the ability of the state actors to intervene in private and market transactions. Tackling the problem of corruption, or the abuse of public trust for private gain, is not possible by simply jailing corrupt individuals without changing the incentives for corruption. It is imperative to create a constitution with checks and balances and rule of law. Where corruption exists, the effects typically fall disproportionately on the poor, since the cost of bribes is felt more severely by the poor than by the rich, and on small firms, since they feel the pinch more than large firms do (Figure 7.2).

Overall, the reasons that states with poor governance fail stem from many factors. Failing states may be more rigid in decision making, and they may lack the capability to administer detailed plans. Bureaucratic obstacles may block private-sector initiatives and innovation. It is hard to replicate a private-market incentive system within a govern-

Figure 7.2 Disproportionate Effects of Corruption on Small vs. Large Firms and on Poor vs. High-Income Households

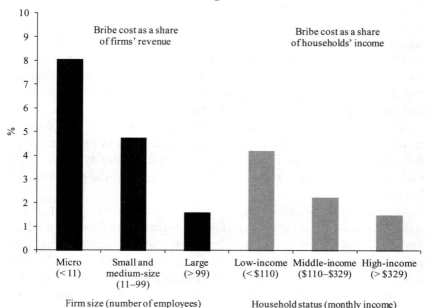

SOURCE: Kaufmann, Zoido-Lobatón, and Lee (2000).

ment. Branches of government may also be poorly coordinated and lack effective oversight. Excessive state controls may cause black markets to expand through increased incentives for rent seeking and corruption.

Development planning may be manipulated by small, privileged groups for their own benefit. Combinations of the above factors make it very difficult for a state to function effectively and to maintain a sense of societal order.

BUILDING POLITICAL AND ECONOMIC INSTITUTIONS FOR GOOD GOVERNANCE

Effective and inclusive institutions provide "rules of the political and economic game" of human interaction. They provide foundations of a market economy, including secured property and land rights, contract enforcement, economic coordination, restriction of coercive or fraudulent behavior, and provision of access to opportunities for the broad participation of citizens. They do this by constraining the opportunist power of elites through the use of checks and balances. Successful governance includes managing conflict, providing social insurance, and fostering predictable macroeconomic stability. The conditions of well-functioning, inclusive market institutions for good governance include the following: clear and secured property rights, effective laws and courts, freedom to establish businesses, a stable currency, public supervision of natural monopolies to manage externalities (i.e., positive or negative spillover effects), transparent provision of credible public information to citizens, stable monetary and fiscal policy instruments, and social safety nets for those on the street, such as the homeless and beggars.

Political parties are necessary but not sufficient for good governance. No society can expect stability and democracy in a place where autocratic government derives its power through ethnically, racially, or religiously exclusive membership motivated by divide-and-rule politics. The historic experiences of countries and societies who have ruled by such groupings make this clear. A case in point in Africa was a racial or ethnic minority-rule system known as "apartheid," which collapsed in South Africa in 1994 after having created serious socioeconomic

The Challenges of Good Governance in Developing Countries 143

inequality in wealth and education. South Africa today is struggling to be a multiethnic democratic state and to overcome that legacy of divide-and-rule. Although the majority-black South Africans may have political power because of free elections, the legacy of income and wealth inequality persists and contributes to serious property-related crimes, such as violent robbery and murder along racial and ethnic lines.

Social science studies show that the best way to manage a potential ethnic conflict is through a representative civic-based democracy, one that is open to inclusive participation of citizens in politics. In such an open democratic society, Barack Obama, a man with roots in Africa, has risen to become president of the most powerful democratic nation in the world, in a place where much wealth was created through African enslavement.

In Eastern Europe, the former Soviet state of Yugoslavia collapsed amid ethnic and political conflict. Yugoslavia, under former president Josip Broz Tito, was a viable and progressive Eastern European state before its own collapse and the collapse of the former Soviet Union in 1991. But when ethnic and religious identity politics were unleashed after the fall of Tito, a vicious ethnic civil war took place, in which the Serbs engaged in ethnic cleansing against Muslims. This was eventually stopped only by the intervention of European powers, led by the United States. Nevertheless, the damaging politics of ethnic and religious identity took their toll. "Revolutionary democracy" is a term that has sometimes been applied to the Balkan conflict, as well as to unrest in Egypt and Ethiopia, but there is no such thing as "revolutionary democracy" in practice, since democracy by its very nature is evolutionary. Democracy is a result of civilized compromise among responsible citizens and politicians over key policies and issues of human development at both the national and local levels. Social democracy, such as the governing system in Sweden, requires a highly educated population with highly developed human capital and takes a long time to achieve. It is unlikely to work in an income-poor country with no middle class or a weak private sector and civil society, and where ethnic and religious conflicts are unsettled. Liberal democracy, adapted to local culture, has the best chance of giving political choices to citizens if two things happen. First, it must be promoted from the bottom up. Second, a middle class economy must grow up to support a strong civic society and private sector. A country in Africa that has effectively adopted liberal democracy is Botswana.

Botswana today has the best-rated governance on the continent, with the best-managed economy and minimal corruption, resulting in the top per-capita income and Human Development Index in Africa. There are others, such as Ghana, Tanzania, Mozambique, Malawi, Benin, and Senegal, that are moving forward along this line. Multiethnic developing countries such as India, Malaysia, and South Africa have opened to democratic majority rule. Ethiopia must learn from these large multiethnic countries. A model for Ethiopia may be India, a large multiethnic Asian country that achieved democratic unity under ethnic and religious diversity, and whose political leaders are freely elected in competitive national and local elections. India's democracy, given its ethnic and religious diversity, has allowed the country to become an emerging economic giant that may compete with China, where political freedom is comparatively less.

Most African rulers oppose liberal democracy for self-serving reasons, since this form of democracy erodes their monopolistic power and forces them to compete and compromise, provided there are checks and balances provided by democratic institutions. "Democratic institutions" are legal and constitutional entities that provide checks on power, such as a free press, an independent judiciary, and competing parties loyal to the nation or its people, with term limits on key power holders. Amartya K. Sen, the Indian Nobel laureate in development economics, was correct when he wrote that "no famine has historically taken place in a country with a free press" (Sen 2006, p. 34).

There are few countries that practice liberal democracy in Africa. As mentioned above, a rare example is Botswana, which is the most economically developed and well-governed country on the continent, with the highest per-capita income, at $8,000 a year, and the highest human development index (HDI) in Africa. HDI is a composite index of quality of human life that includes income, education, and health. Botswana today is the beneficiary of hundreds of medical and health professionals from Ethiopia and other African countries because of its democratic good governance. Botswana used wealth from diamonds to enhance human development and avoided the "resource curse" problem (the tendency for the finding of rich deposits of mineral resources in a country governed badly or by a dictator to lead to strife and corrup-

The Challenges of Good Governance in Developing Countries 145

tion in that country over control of the resource), whereas other African countries, such as Sierra Leone, Nigeria, Sudan, Liberia, and the Congo, have suffered from conflicts fought over natural resources.

Botswana stands tall next to neighboring Zimbabwe, which is in shambles because of the abuse of power. Its president, Robert Mugabe, is a 91-year-old dictator who refuses to yield power by accepting defeat by the opposition in the last election, and who has held onto rule for 28 years. Zimbabwe is one of the saddest cases of abuse of power by long-term, one-man rule in Africa. Mugabe continues to blame the country's one-time British colonial masters in the former Rhodesia for what is actually damage inflicted by his own government on the people of Zimbabwe. Mugabe could have used his power to make early political and economic reforms, such as land reform. However, in 1988, shortly after taking office, he abolished the main opposition party, headed by former independence fighter Joshua Nokomo, and formed a monopoly, his Zimbabwe African National Union (ZANU) party.

The British colonial rulers departed from Zimbabwe in 1980, leaving the country with a modern infrastructure of standards close to those of Europe, including a vibrant agricultural economy that produced surplus food crops such as maize. The agriculture was based on modern farms and gave food aid to Ethiopia during the famine of 1984–1985. But after Mugabe and his associates took power in 1987, their policies wreaked havoc on Zimbabwe's agricultural economy and its human capital assets. Today, Zimbabwe's economy is destroyed and its currency is worthless; the country has abandoned its national currency and is now using U.S. dollars. Millions of citizens are exiled as refugees to border countries such as Botswana and South Africa.

In general, ethnic-, clan-, and religious-based political parties are not viable in promoting democracy or good governance. They are likely to create both intraethnic and interethnic political conflicts. They cannot be democratic by the very nature of their formation, since they are exclusive and prone to conflict, both within themselves and with other ethnic parties. For example, each ethnic party in Ethiopia today is split into two or more antagonistic groups, which are variously either aligned with the ruling party, exiled, or in rebellion. In contrast, enlightened political leaders can provide effective leadership in cooperation with other multiethnic nationals.

Political groups that continue to exploit the divisions that emerge with the breakup of large African states are likely to create massive destruction. Doing so could risk all that has been built up through the centuries by the successful historic evolution into a nation state. One example is the state of Ethiopia, with its ancient civilization. Ethiopia was the only African country never colonized by European powers. For politicians and leaders, the challenge is to bridge these deep historical and cultural connections for the benefit of all. To act in the narrow interests of one's party can lead to failure. Consider what occurred in Egypt, for example, where the recently elected government of the Islamic Brotherhood, led by President Mohamed Morsi, was overthrown by the combined forces of the military and the citizenry. One reason for his party's failure is that it was not perceived as being inclusive of all Egyptians, such as women, based on its name. Indeed, the very name connotes religious affiliation, which may have caused Egyptians to fear that Morsi would turn Egypt into an Iranian Islamic–style theocracy. Regardless of policy, parties based on religious, ethnic, or clan affiliations will fail in any nonhomogeneous society by creating a divisive environment. Political parties must be inclusive of all citizens in order to succeed.

Elections are a necessary but not a sufficient condition for good governance. Today, the overwhelming majority of Africans strive for better education and health, and they yearn to be free from top-down rule by the political elite. In Ethiopia, there was the experiment of ethnic federalism imposed from the top; this system uses the institutions of the former totalitarian state of the military dictator Col. Mengistu Haile Mariam, which collapsed in 1991 (Mariam 2011).

Ethnic federalism is a form of federalism based on dividing a country along ethnic and linguistic lines. It retards market integration and communication among citizens that share a common culture and heritage. There are powerful pan-Ethiopian traits among the 80-some ethnic groups in Ethiopia, but these traits have been compromised since the 1991 collapse of rule of the military junta. The vast majority of Ethiopians, about 85 percent, make their livelihood in agriculture and want security of land so they can engage in land transactions and use land as collateral to get credits or loans. They desire to be real owners of their landholdings and to get necessary improved inputs, training, credit, agricultural extension, marketing, and technology to improve agricultural and food productivity. However, they cannot get credit, since they do not meet the legal requirement of land ownership, which would allow them to use land as collateral to get loans. In other developing countries such as South Korea, Taiwan, Japan, and India, private ownership of farmland and flexible free land transactions, including tenancy, have been properly regulated under the rule of law and have created agricultural revolutions. This has transformed agriculture not only by attracting capital and technology but by optimizing farm sizes through flexible markets that promote equity and agricultural productivity and protect natural resource degradation.

GOOD GOVERNANCE FOR EFFECTIVE GLOBAL ENGAGEMENT, FOREIGN INVESTMENT, AID, AND TRADE

All African states, including Ethiopia, can benefit from the kind of good governance that fosters effective regional and global engagement and cooperation. The second-most populated African state, Ethiopia is home to the African Union, the Economic Community of Africa, and a large diplomatic community of national embassies and international organizations such as United Nations offices, as well as nongovernmental organizations, or NGOs. Using good governance, Ethiopia can improve relations with other regional powers, particularly countries in Africa, Asia, and the Middle East. Good governance in Ethiopia and attempts to reach out to these other powers will help prevent conflict driven by dictatorships, assuming the partners also practice good governance.

Since it is landlocked because of the breakaway by Eritrea in 1993, Ethiopia could benefit by promoting good trade relations and cross-border movement of people, commodities, and investment, as well as promoting the regional public good through human security.

For instance, a positive relationship and trade with Somalia would open up the coastline of Africa all along the Indian Ocean for the benefit of both Eritrea and Ethiopia and the entire Horn of Africa.

Furthermore, Ethiopia and other African states can use their large diaspora population of skilled individuals, who can constructively engage their homeland through remittances, investment, and transferring knowledge and skills through creative academic and business partnership programs. If the diaspora can be enlisted in this way, a major source of human capital will be created that can inject investment and knowledge into all sectors of the economy. Moreover, the diaspora should be encouraged to invest beyond just bonds, into areas such as dam construction, banks, insurance companies, and other sectors like industry, tourism, information technology, and agriculture.

Since around 1991, with the end of the Cold War, some African states, including Ethiopia, opened up to the West and Asia, including the Middle East, North America, and Europe. This reestablished the strong historic U.S.-Ethiopia tie that had been interrupted during the rule of the Soviet-influenced military junta between 1974 and 1991.

It is important to remember that, until the time of the junta, the U.S.-Ethiopia partnership was strongly beneficial for both countries from its beginning in 1903, during the presidency of Theodore Roosevelt, through the next 70 years. Strong national organizations, such as Ethiopian Airlines and the defense forces, including the air force and the navy, benefited from this partnership, which included a large Peace Corps contingent and student exchange programs from which Ethiopians of that generation benefited in terms of a high-quality education. Ethiopia was respected in Africa and throughout the world. The nation was relatively peaceful and united until 1974, when Ethiopia fell under the sway of Soviet Cold War geopolitics and was taken over by a military junta. This junta collapsed in 1991, the same year that the Soviet Union did. It may be possible to reestablish that former U.S. partnership through creative exchanges between Americans and Ethiopians with genuine leadership on both sides. Current and future U.S. governments should invest more in helping to build good governance, institutions for democracy, education, peace, and conflict resolution in Ethiopia, as well as high-quality education and improvements in human rights. Ethiopian academics from the diaspora can transform education and health if allowed an opportunity to do so under creative partnerships.

In terms of the relationship between economic development and foreign aid, there are three main perspectives scholars have expressed on the way foreign aid affects development. The first is that foreign aid has an overall positive impact on economic development, with some exceptions. The second is that aid has little or no effect on development, and in some cases may actually be a hindrance. For example,

The Challenges of Good Governance in Developing Countries   149

the effect of food aid lowers domestic food prices and displaces local food production. The third perspective sees the effect of foreign aid as conditional on the level of good governance. For instance, aid has been beneficial to countries like Botswana, where good governance is high. However, Table 7.4 shows that African countries attract by far the largest amount of global aid, both in dollar amount and in percentage of GDP, and yet that aid has not translated into economic progress. For example, food aid creates dependency by reducing local food production. In particular, the food aid accepted by Ethiopia has impaired that country's local agriculture and food production; consequently, it stands to reason that accepting such aid should be avoided unless there is an emergency.

Ethiopia ranks just above Zimbabwe and below Liberia in the 2012 Legatum Index, a comprehensive measure of governance that includes eight broad indicators of human progress: 1) economy, 2) entrepreneurship opportunity, 3) governance, 4) education, 5) health, 6) safety, 7) personal freedom, and 8) social capital. The complex contributors to low investment and entrepreneurship include corruption, low human capital, fiscal instability, bad infrastructure, low levels of domestic savings, and poor coordination. By enabling entrepreneurship, good governance helps to overcome the lack of productivity from the low investment trap.

Table 7.4 Global and Regional Foreign Aid Distribution

	Millions of US$	Percent of GDP	Dollars per person
Sub-Saharan Africa	24,144	6.0	34
South Asia	6,169	0.8	4
East Asia and Pacific	7,140	0.4	4
Europe and Central Asia	10,465	0.8	22
Middle East and North Africa	7,628	1.0	24
Latin America and Caribbean	6,153	0.4	12
Low income	32,135	3.0	14
Lower-middle income	21,775	0.5	8
Upper-middle income	3,778	0.2	11
High income	1,273	0.0	1

World Bank (2014).

THE CASE OF CHINA—EXCEPTION TO THE RULE?

In the past three decades China has made impressive economic progress, exhibiting stellar economic growth rates coupled with a significant reduction in poverty and rapid advances in many human development dimensions. On the surface, it seems that China has achieved good governance outcomes even while defying those criteria or indices of good governance mentioned in our earlier analysis and delineated by the World Bank and other organizations. Especially in the areas of voice and accountability and the rule of law, it does seem that China does not meet the criteria of good governance. In addition, the China case appears to counter the common prescriptions that development scholars recommend to developing countries for successful governance and for avoiding potential ethnic conflict and instability—namely, to pursue a liberal democratic institution that is representative and open to the inclusive participation of citizens in politics.

Indeed, China is ruled by an authoritarian regime governed by a single party (the Chinese Communist Party, or CCP) that restricts and suppresses civic participation and elections, political freedom of expression and assembly, and freedom of the press.

However, if we examine the case of China more carefully, we find the principle of voice and accountability actually exists, and that of the rule of law as well, only in different forms rooted in Chinese culture and its long history and civilization. Zhang Weiwei, director of the Center for China Development Model Research, Fudan University, and director of the Institute of China Studies, Shanghai Academy of Social Sciences, argues that China practices economic accountability. Government in China, at all levels, is held accountable for promoting economic growth and job creation, Weiwei (2014) contends, since an official cannot be promoted unless the area under his governance performs well economically.

There is also political and legal accountability (and, to the extent of such accountability, rule of law) because the officials are held accountable and demoted or punished for accidents, such as fires that could have been averted by following proper precautions and regulations. Other crimes, disasters, missteps, policy mistakes, and corruption cases are routinely being exposed.

The Challenges of Good Governance in Developing Countries   151

Weiwei also points out that China's neodemocratic centralism may have some advantage over a collective decision-making process in terms of governing effectiveness. China has institutionalized a procedural accountability for its democratic centralism. Under such a system, a major decision like determining the nation's five-year plan for development takes well over a year of extensive and interactive consultations at various levels of the Chinese state and society. This decision-making process receives inputs from thousands of think tanks, government agencies, universities, prominent scholars, and professionals. The recently adopted decision by the Third Plenum on deepening reforms is a good example in this regard. China's socioeconomic plan-drafting group, chaired by President Xi Jinping himself, solicited opinions from well over 100 institutions across the country and received 2,500 suggestions over a period of six months. About half of these suggestions were accepted. During the consultation process, all of the nation's seven top leaders travel to different regions and provinces of China to make investigations in preparation for the deliberations on the final decision and to learn the opinions of local people. As a result, the decision reflects the broad consensus of Chinese society on many issues such as public health reform, adjustment of the one-child policy, deferred retirement age, banking sector reform, and education reform. China's system of accountability performs better than that of most states around the world, and it achieves this in a country that is rapidly moving toward becoming the world's largest economy in the twenty-first century.

SUMMARY AND CONCLUSION

Good governance for sustainable human development is a multidimensional process involving socioeconomic and political transformation of societies; it is aimed at enhancing human progress in all its dimensions, including freedom of political and economic choice. A program of good governance, along with education on how to achieve peaceful transformation and conflict resolution, should be instituted across schools, universities, and colleges to teach citizenship, the qualities of a civil society, and responsible ethical conduct.

In their book *Why Nations Fail*, mentioned in the introduction, the leading institutional economists at the Massachusetts Institute of Technology, Daron Acemoglu and James Robinson, examine the stark contrast in living conditions between the two Koreas, North and South, and also delve into the reasons why Botswana has risen while its neighbor, Zimbabwe, is sinking. Beyond that, Acemoglu and Robinson (2011), looking toward the future, give suggestions for ways in which larger nations like the United States and China can build more sustainable and egalitarian political and economic institutions.

While the issues involved in bringing about positive changes in countries are complex, positive economic development does not in fact have a secret formula. Simply put, successful development requires good governance. Positive instances can be found in East Asia, Europe, North America, and elsewhere. Unfortunately, Botswana is one of the few examples of development through good governance in Africa. The question remains: why have African countries lagged behind other developing nations, such as those of Asia? It is not for lack of natural resources, good climate, or a hard-working people. Most African states plagued by poverty suffer because of government repression. These leaders rely on the instruments of fear and coercion to prevent honest dialogue and freedom of expression. They have, by and large, failed to learn the lessons of the past, both from their own history and from that of successful nations. We hope political leaders will make a different, positive choice, one of building inclusive economic, political, and social institutions in the twenty-first century. The single comprehensive factor that can take Africa as well as states in Asia, the Middle East, and Latin America out of poverty and conflict is democratic good governance, which will positively affect all sectors of the economy.

References

Acemoglu, Daron, and James A. Robinson. 2011. Why *Nations Fail: The Origins of Power, Prosperity, and Poverty.* New York: Random House.

Collier, Paul. 2007. *The Bottom Billion: Why the Poorest Countries Are Failing and What Can Be Done about It.* New York: Oxford University Press.

Gates, Melinda. 2014. "How Boko Haram Imperils Nigeria's Future." CNN.com, May 9. http://www.cnn.com/2014/05/08/opinion/gates-boko-haram-nigeria-girls/ (accessed February 17, 2015).

Kaufmann, Daniel. 2010. *Governance Matters*. Washington, DC: Brookings Institution.

Kaufmann, Daniel, Pablo Zoido-Lobatón, and Young Lee. 2000. *Governance and Anticorruption Diagnostic Study for Ecuador*. Washington, DC: World Bank Institute.

Mariam, Al. 2011. "Why Is Ethiopia Poor?" (blog). http://open.salon.com/blog/almariam/2011/11/27/why_is_ethiopia_poor (accessed February 18, 2015).

Myrdal, Gunnar. 1968. *Asian Drama*. New York: Pantheon.

Ostrom, Elinor. 1990. *Governing the Commons: The Evolution of Institutions for Collective Action*. Cambridge: Cambridge University Press.

Rotberg, Robert I., and Rachel M. Gisselquist. 2007. *Strengthening African Governance: Ibrahim Index of African Governance, Results and Rankings 2007*. Somerville, MA: World Peace Foundation, Fletcher School, Tufts University.

Sen, Amartya K. 2006. *Identity and Violence: The Illusion of Destiny*. New York: Norton.

Todaro, Michael P., and Stephen C. Smith. 2014. *Economic Development*. 12th ed. Pearson Series in Economics. Upper Saddle River, NJ: Prentice Hall.

Weiwei, Zhang. 2014. "The Five Reasons Why China Works." *World Post*, February 26. www.huffingtonpost.com/zhang-weiwei/the-five-reasons-china-works_b_4859899.html (accessed April 6, 2015).

World Bank. 2014. *Worldwide Governance Indicators*. Washington, DC: World Bank. http://info.worldbank.org/governance/wgi/index.aspx#home (accessed April 3, 2015).

Authors

Sisay Asefa is a professor of economics and director of the Center for African Development Policy Research at Western Michigan University. His research interests include the political economy of poverty, food security, rural development, and governance and institutions.

Carolyn J. Heinrich is the Sid Richardson Professor of Public Affairs and affiliated professor of economics and the director of the Center for Health and Social Policy at the Lyndon B. Johnson School of Public Affairs, University of Texas at Austin. She collaborates with nongovernmental organizations such as the World Bank, the Inter-American Development Bank, and UNICEF in research to improve program and policy design and the impacts and effectiveness of economic and social investments in middle-income and developing countries.

Wei-Chiao Huang is a professor in the Department of Economics at Western Michigan University. His research interests comprise labor economics and applied microeconomics, including brain drain, the economics of immigration, and various issues related to China's economic reforms.

John Ishiyama is a University Distinguished Research Professor of Political Science at the University of North Texas. His research interests include democratization; political parties; Ethiopia; and postcommunist Russian, eastern European, and central Asian politics.

Seema Jayachandran is an associate professor of economics and director of the Center for the Study of Development Economics at Northwestern University. Her research focuses on economic issues in developing countries, including the determinants of parents' investments in their children's health and education.

Susan J. Linz is a professor of economics at Michigan State University. She looks at economic transition, changing labor market conditions, business and economic conditions, entrepreneurship, and the influence of personality traits and attitudes on employee performance.

Stephen C. Smith is a professor of economics and international affairs in the Elliott School of International Affairs at George Washington University, a nonresident senior fellow at the Brookings Institution in Washington, D.C., and a research fellow at the Institute for the Study of Labor (IZA) in Bonn, Germany. He directs George Washington University's Research Program in Poverty, Development, and Globalization. His work focuses on economic development, with a special focus on solutions to poverty.

Index

Note: The italic letters *f, n,* or *t* following a page number indicate a figure, note, or table on that page. Double letters mean more than one such item on a single page.

ACA (Patient Protection and Affordable Care Act, 2010), 2, 20–21
Accountability, 7
  as aspect of good governance, 4, 6, 12, 53, 132*f*
  educational, with rigid definitions based on factory-model approach, 3, 22, 25–26
  grants-in-aid and, 104, 107*n*1
  paired with voice as aspect of good governance, 1, 57, 60, 61*f,* 71, 71*f,* 87*n*14, 131, 150
  political and legal, by government officials, 150–151
Acemoglu, Daron, coauthor of *Why Nations Fail*, 11, 152
Adaptation, 111
  climate change, and conflict risk, 121–122, 123–125
  planned, and public policy, 122–125
Adverse selection, in agency theory, 18
Affordable Care Act (ACA, 2010), 2, 20–21
Afghanistan, preventable mortality in, 10, 114
Africa, 112
  challenges of good governance and leadership in, 11–13, 125
  European colonization of, 12, 145, 146
  governance measures in, 133, 136*t,* 137*t*
  poverty in, 112, 113, 136*t,* 137
  poverty reduction in, 9, 152
  preventable mortality in, 10, 114
  regional state groupings in, 113, 147, 149*t*
  21st century, and governance choices, 13, 146, 152
  See also names of individual states, e.g., Ethiopia; Zimbabwe

African Union, 125, 147
Agency theory
  complexity of values and goals in, 2–3, 20, 22, 30–31*n*2
  roots of performance management in, 17–18
Agricultural factors, 113, 116
  climate change and farmers *vs.* herdsmen, 123, 124
  land erosion and overuse, 118, 140
  land ownership and reform, 59, 137, 140, 146–147
Albania
  as a CEE country, 7, 86*n*13
  corruption in, 64*f,* 76*f*
  governance measures in, 67*f,* 69*f,* 72*f,* 74*f,* 77*f*
Angola
  IIAG scores for, 136, 137*t*
  MPI and income poverty for, 133, 135*t*
Annan, U.N. Sec. Gen. Kofi, 10, 114
Apartheid, as exclusive politics, 142
Arab Spring, 5
Armenia
  as an FSU country, 7, 86*n*12
  corruption in, 64*f,* 76*f*
  governance measures in, 66*f,* 68*f,* 70*f,* 72*f,* 73*f,* 77*f*
Asia, 113, 149*t*
  challenges of good governance and leadership in, 11–12
  poverty reduction in, 9, 152
  preventable mortality in, 10, 114
  See also names of individual states, e.g., China; India
Autocracies, 5, 6, 146
Azerbaijan
  as an FSU country, 7, 86*n*12
  corruption in, 64*f,* 76*f*

158 Asefa and Huang

Azerbaijan, *cont.*
  governance measures in, 66*f,* 68*f,* 70*f,*
    72*f,* 73*f,* 77*f*

Balkan conflict. *See* Yugoslavia
Baltic republics. *See* Estonia; Latvia;
  Lithuania
Bangladesh, 134*t*
  climate migrants and violence in, 123,
    124
BEEPS. *See* Business Environment and
  Enterprise Performance Survey
Belarus
  as an FSU country, 7, 86*n*12
  corruption in, 64*f,* 76*f*
  governance measures in, 66*f,* 68*f,* 70*f,*
    72*f,* 73*f,* 77*f*
Benin, 144
  IIAG scores for, 136, 137*t*
Bobbit, Franklin, 25
Bolivia, MPI and income poverty for,
  134*t*
Bosnia-Herzegovina, 7, 76*f,* 86*n*13
  IEF in, 77*f*
Botswana, 145
  governance and poverty measures
    compared for selected African
    countries, 133, 136*t*
  governance measures in, 131, 136,
    137*t,* 144, 149
  government of, contrasted with
    Zimbabwe, 11–12, 152
Brazil, MPI and income poverty for, 134*t*
Bribery, 7–8, 62, 88*n*25
  as business and household problem,
    141, 141*f*
  in CEE compared to FSU countries,
    79–80, 80*f,* 81*ff*
  as education and health care
    governance problems, 96, 97
Britain, African colonization by, 12, 145
Bulgaria
  as a CEE country, 7, 86*n*13
  corruption in, 64*f,* 76*f*
  governance measures in, 67*f,* 69*f,* 70*f,*
    72*f,* 74*f,* 77*f*

Bureaucracy, time taxes in, 7, 80, 82*f*
Burkina Faso, IIAG scores for, 136, 137*t*
Burundi, IIAG scores for, 136, 137*t*
Business Environment and Enterprise
  Performance Survey (BEEPS)
  as governance measurement, 6, 58,
    86*n*10
  summary of, data in transition
    economies, 77–80, 78*f,* 79*f,* 80*f,*
    81*ff,* 82*ff,* 83*f*
Business firms, 16, 149
  corruption's cost to, 62, 79–80, 141,
    141*f*
  perspective of, on transitional
    economies, 6, 7

Cameroon, IIAG scores for, 136, 137*t*
Cape Verde, IIAG scores for, 136, 137*t*
Capital, credit for, 10, 117–118, 119,
  139, 147
CCP (Chinese Communist Party), 150
CEE countries. *See* Central and Eastern
  European countries
Central African Republic, IIAG scores
  for, 136, 137*t*
Central and Eastern European (CEE)
  countries
  control of corruption in, 61*f,* 62–65,
    63*f,* 64*f,* 87*nn*18–19
  transition economies in, 6–7, 59–60,
    86*nn*12–13
  WGI scores in, 60, 61*f,* 87*nn*14–15
  See also names of individual states,
    e.g., Albania; Poland
Central and Eastern European (CEE)
  countries, compared to FSU
  countries
  bribery in, 79–80, 80*f,* 81*ff*
  corruption as obstacle in, 78–80, 78*f,*
    79*f,* 83*f*
  CPI in, 75, 76*f*
  Freedom House governance measures
    in, 74, 75*f*
  government effectiveness in, 65, 66*f*
  IEF in, 75–76, 77*f*

Central and Eastern European (CEE)
countries, compared to FSU
countries, *cont.*
  obstacles facing firms in, 84*f*
  permit applications in, 78, 80, 82*f,*
    83*f,* 85*f*
  political stability in, 71, 73*f,* 74
  regulatory quality in, 65, 67*f,* 68
  rule of law in, 68, 69*f,* 71
  tax regulation in, 80, 82*f*
  voice and accountability in, 60, 61*f,*
    71, 71*f*
  WGI scores in, 60, 61*f,* 63*f,* 66*f,* 67*f,*
    69*f,* 71*f,* 73*f*
Chad
  IIAG scores for, 136, 137*t*
  preventable mortality in, 10, 114
Child welfare systems, 2, 28
  unintended consequences of market-
    based incentives for, 21–22
Children, 26, 151
  as laborers or slaves, 115, 139
  mortality of, as health measurement,
    10, 114, 132
  as refugees, 120
China, 112, 134*t,* 144, 152
  governance in, as exception to rule,
    150–151
  health care providers and perverse
    incentives in, 99–100
  outcomes of one-party state in, 4, 12,
    150
Chinese Communist Party (CCP), as
    authoritarian regime, 150
Citizenry, 11
  empowerment of, 104–106, 119
  hierarchical relationships of, 20, 24
  human rights of, 6, 133
  interaction of, fostered by good
    governance, 1, 6, 53, 136
  needs of, and responsive institutions,
    132, 151
  objectives of, 2, 15, 20
Civil liberties, 150
  Freedom House survey of, 57, 74

as governance measurement, 6, 75*f,*
  132
Civil wars
  drivers of, 117, 121, 138, 143
  government effectiveness and, 42, 43,
    43*t,* 44, 44*t,* 45*t*
Cleveland, Harlan, 15, 30*n*1
Climate change, 113, 116
  adapting to, and conflict risk, 121–
    122, 123–125
  importance of addressing, with good
    governance, 13, 123–126
  poverty reduction and, 8–10
Colombia, MPI and income poverty for,
  134*t*
Comoros, IIAG scores for, 136, 137*t*
CompStat/CitiStat model, performance
  management data and, 29–30
Conflict, 151
  capital development destroyed by,
    120–121
  consequences of, 119–120
  drivers of, 11, 121, 125, 138–140,
    142–143, 147
  poverty and, 111, 112, 152
  risk of, and climate change
    adaptations, 121–122, 123–125
  trap of, 117, 138
Congo, Democratic Republic of, 10, 120,
  145
  IIAG scores (grades C and F) for,
    136, 137*t*
  MPI and income poverty for, 133, 135*t*
Corruption
  business firm's perspective on, 7, 77–
    78, 86*n*11, 87*nn*16–17, 88*nn*24–26
  control measurements for, 5, 40, 56,
    60, 61*f,* 76–77, 87*n*15
  control of, as aspect of good
    governance, 1, 6, 46, 63*f,* 64*ff,* 140
  developing countries and, 7–8, 60–65,
    140–142
  as IIAG component, 133, 136
  as obstacle in CEE compared to FSU
    countries, 78–80, 78*f,* 79*f,* 88*n*27

160 Asefa and Huang

Corruption, *cont.*
  political parties and, 4–5, 35, 46
  poor governance as driver of, traps, 11, 140–142
  post–civil war states and, 43, 44
Corruption Perceptions Index (CPI)
  in CEE compared to FSU countries, 75, 76*f*
  compared to HDI, IIAG, MPI for selected African countries, 133, 136*t*
  as governance measurement, 6, 7, 57, 86*n*7
Côte d'Ivoire, MPI and income poverty for, 135*t*
CPI. *See* Corruption Perceptions Index
Croatia
  as a CEE country, 7, 86*n*13
  corruption in, 64*f,* 76*f*
  governance measures in, 67*f,* 69*f,* 70*f,* 72*f,* 74*f,* 77*f*
Cultural factors
  governance shaped by, 150–151
  kinship and reciprocity as, and institutional corruption, 59, 62–63, 84
Czech Republic, 59
  as a CEE country, 7, 86*n*13
  corruption in, 64*f,* 76*f*
  governance measures in, 67*f,* 69*f,* 70*f,* 72*f,* 74*f,* 77*f*

Darfur, causes of conflict in, 121
Democracies
  conflict management in, 142, 143
  decision making in, 12, 53–54, 144, 151
  designing performance management in, 2, 16
  good governance and, 6, 13, 42, 142, 145, 150
  political parties' influence in, 4–6, 35
  types of, 12, 143, 150–151
Denmark, high standard of governance in, 131

Developing countries, 8
  education and health care in (*see* Education in developing countries; Health care in developing countries)
  good governance and leadership challenges in, 10–13, 122, 131–152
  impacts of climate change on, 121–122
  international aid to, 46, 52, 86*n*2
  mortality rates in, 10, 114
  political parties' influence on democracy in, 4–6, 35–47
Digital technology, performance management and, 26, 104
Djibouti, 136, 136*t,* 137*t*
Dominican Republic, MPI and income poverty for, 134*t*
Downs, Anthony, 47*n*1
Dropout rates, U.S. education and, 3–4
Duncan, U.S. Sec. of Educ. Arne, 19
Dynamics of Performance Management, The (Moynihan), 15–16

Economic accountability, China and, 150
Economic Community of Africa, 147
Economic development
  components of, 136–137
  corruption's effect on, 61–62
  foreign aid and, 148–149
  good governance required for, 12–13, 51, 86*n*1, 112
Economic freedom, 151
  index of, 57–58, 86*nn*8–9
Economic growth, 54, 112, 150
  in Asia contrasted with Africa, 12, 152
  government failure and, 111, 115
  promoted by education and health, 93, 107
  transitional governments and, 6, 41, 43*t,* 44*t,* 45*t*
Economist Intelligence Unit (organization), 58
Ecuador, MPI and income poverty for, 134*t*

Education
  as component of human development
    indexes, 136, 149
  foreign, of U.S. immigrants and dollar
    value, 94–95
  importance of, to good governance,
    13, 100–101
  MPI measurements of, 114, 132
  service deliveries for, and public
    sector agencies, 21, 22–24
Education in developing countries
  economic growth and, 93, 107
  governance challenges and, 93–101
  indicators of, 94–95, 112
  money for, 7–8, 93, 96–97, 107
  problems addressed, 94, 102–103,
    104, 105–106
  problems encountered, 96–97, 98–99,
    100–101, 107
  quality issues, 94–95, 96, 100–101,
    105, 106, 107, 138
Education reform
  factors in failure of, 3–4, 8, 23–25
  NCLB and, 19, 25–26
  proposals for, 11, 26–27, 151
Egypt, political unrest in, 5, 143, 146
Elementary and Secondary Education
    Act (ESEA, 2002), 24, 25
Entrepreneurial opportunity, 149
Environment (business). *See* Business
    Environment and Performance
    Survey (BEEPS)
Environment (geophysical), 28
  degradation or stress on, as poverty
    cause/trap, 111, 118, 139–140
  federal agencies on, 30–31*n*2
  impact of climate change in, on
    poverty reduction, 8–10
  See also Natural resources
EPA (U.S. Environmental Protection
    Agency), 30–31*n*2
Equatorial Guinea, IIAG scores for, 136,
    137*t*
Equity, as aspect of good governance,
    6, 53
Eritrea, 147

governance and poverty in, 133, 136*t*
IIAG scores for, 136, 137*t*
ESEA (Elementary and Secondary
    Education Act, 2002), 24, 25
Estonia, 74
  corruption in, 64*f,* 75, 76*f*
  as either a CEE or FSU country, 7,
    86*n*12
  governance measures in, 66*f,* 68*f,* 70*f,*
    71, 72*f,* 73*f,* 77*f*
Ethics, 18, 151
  complexity of values and goals in
    agency theory, 2–3, 20, 30–31*n*2
Ethiopia
  conflict vulnerability in, 138, 143
  famine in, and food aid, 145, 149
  farm traps and poverty in, 118, 137–
    138, 139
  governance and poverty measures
    compared for selected African
    countries, 133, 136*t*
  IIAG scores for, 136, 137*t*
  MPI and income poverty for, 133,
    135*t*
  political models for, 144, 146–147
  property rights in, 140, 146
  regional cooperatives and, 147–149
Ethiopian Airlines, 148
Ethnicity
  as driver of conflict, 138–139, 142–
    143, 145
  as nonviable basis for promoting
    good governance, 145, 146
  in studied transitional economies, 42,
    43*t,* 44*t,* 45*t*
Europe
  regional recipients of foreign aid in,
    149*t*
  See also Central and Eastern
    European (CEE) countries;
    European Union (EU); *names of
    individual states, e.g.* France
European Bank for Reconstruction and
    Development (EBRD)
  BEEPS a collaboration from, 58,
    86*nn*10–11

162 Asefa and Huang

European Bank for Reconstruction and Development (EBRD), *cont.*
 data from, and investment expectations, 52, 86*n*3
European Union (EU), influence of admission requirements, 65, 74

Fertility, poverty traps and, 10, 115, 117, 138
FHI. *See* Freedom House Index
Foreign aid. *See* International assistance
Former Soviet Union (FSU) countries
 control of corruption in, 61*f*, 62–65, 63*f*, 64*f*, 87*nn*18–20
 transitional economies in, 6–7, 59, 86*n*12, 143
 WGI scores in, 60, 61*f*, 87*nn*14–15
 See also names of individual states, e.g., Armenia; Russia
Former Soviet Union (FSU) countries, compared to CEE countries
 bribery in, 79–80, 80*f*, 81*ff*
 corruption seen as obstacle in, 78–80, 78*f*, 79*f*, 83*f*
 CPI in, 75, 76*f*
 Freedom House governance measures in, 74, 75*f*
 government effectiveness in, 65, 66*f*
 IEF in, 75–76, 77*f*
 permit applications in, 78, 80, 82*f*, 83*f*, 85*f*
 political stability in, 71, 73*f*, 74
 regulatory quality in, 65, 67*f*, 68
 rule of law in, 68, 69*f*, 71
 tax regulation in, 80, 82*f*
 voice and accountability in, 60, 61*f*, 71, 71*f*
 WGI scores in, 60, 61*f*, 63*f*, 66*f*, 67*f*, 69*f*, 71*f*, 73*f*
France, 12, 94–95
Freedom aspects, 149
 civil liberties, 6, 57, 74, 75*f*, 132, 150
 economic, 57–58, 86*nn*8–9, 151
 political, 144, 150, 151
Freedom House, annual scores for CEE and FSU countries, 74, 75*f*

Freedom House Index (FHI)
 founders of, organization, 57, 86*n*6
 governance measurements as, 6, 7
FSU countries. *See* Former Soviet Union countries

Gabon, IIAG scores (grades "A" and "F") for, 136, 137*t*
Gambia, IIAG scores for, 136, 137*t*
GDP (gross domestic product), 149*t*
Georgia
 as an FSU country, 7, 86*n*12
 corruption in, 64*f*, 76*f*
 governance measures in, 66*f*, 68*f*, 70*f*, 72*f*, 73*f*, 77*f*
Ghana
 good governance in, 131, 144
 governance and poverty measures compared for, 136, 136*t*, 137*t*
 MPI and income poverty for, 133, 134*t*
Global Integrity Index, 56
GNP (gross national product), 139
Gorsuch, Anne, sought to change agency priorities, 30–31*n*2
Governance, 1, 15, 119, 131
 challenges of, 7–8, 10–13, 93–107, 111–122, 131–152
 economic development dependent on, 12, 112
 good, and aspects of, 1, 6, 27–30, 53, 83–85, 115–116, 122–126, 132*f*, 151
 (*see also under* Transition economies)
 logic of, model and hierarchical relationships, 20, 24
 measurement systems for, 6, 39–40, 55–58, 131, 149
 poor, 11, 13, 76, 125, 133
 relationships of, to development and MPI, 10–11
Government, 4
 effectiveness of, as aspect of good governance, 1, 5, 6, 16, 29–30, 40, 42, 44, 46, 56–57, 65, 66*f*, 87*n*21, 131, 151

Government, *cont.*
efficiency of, as aspect of good
governance, 6, 12, 16, 17
overthrowing, by unconstitutional
means, 5, 46, 146
reinventing, by performance
management, 15–16, 29
roles of, 93, 101, 122
types of, 6, 12, 145–146
Graduation rates, U.S. *vs.* other
countries, 23
Graft, as governance problem, 96–97
Grants-in-aid
accountability and, 104, 107*n*1
prerequisites for, 52, 86*nn*2–4
Green Revolution, 113, 116
Gridlock, political parties and, 4
Gross domestic product (GDP),
percentage of, 149*t*
Gross national product (GNP), highest
in Africa, 139
Guinea, IIAG scores for, 136, 137*t*
Guinea-Bissau
IIAG scores for, 136, 137*t*
preventable mortality in, 10, 114

Haiti, MPI and income poverty for, 135*t*
HDI (Human Development Index), 133,
136*t*, 144
Health, 13, 136
measurements of, 132, 149
poor, as poverty trap, 10, 114, 115,
117, 139
Health care
apply lessons in performance
management to, 28, 30
service deliveries for, 2, 21, 120
Health care in developing countries
governance challenges and, 93–101
indicators of, 94–96, 112
money for, 7–8, 93, 96–97, 107, 120
mortality rates and, 10, 94, 114, 120
problems addressed, 94, 103, 104–
106
problems encountered, 96–101, 107

quality issues, 94, 95–96, 98, 100–101,
105, 106, 107
Health care reform, 2, 8, 20–21, 151
Heritage Foundation, as IEF provider,
57–58, 86*n*8
Hirschman-Herfindahl index, political
party systems and, 40
Housing, inadequate, 10, 117
Human capital
development potential of, 12–13,
132–133
diaspora populations and, 147–148
impact of governance on, in
developing countries, 7–8, 131–
133, 149
Human development, 136
good governance as means to
promote, 131, 147–148, 151–152
measurement and understanding of,
10, 131–133
progress on, 149, 150
Human Development Index (HDI)
compared to CPI, IIAG, MPI for
selected African countries, 133,
136*t*
quality of governance and, 133, 144
Human rights, 6, 133
Hungary, 59
as a CEE country, 7, 86*n*13
corruption in, 64*f*, 76*f*
governance measures in, 67*f*, 69*f*, 70*f*,
72*f*, 74*f*, 77*f*
Hunger, 112
as dimension of poverty, 114, 139
food aid and, 145, 149

Ibrahim Index of African Governance
(IIAG)
compared to CPI, HDI, MPI for
selected countries, 133, 136*t*
core components of, 133, 136
IEF (Index of Economic Freedom),
57–58, 86*nn*8–9
IIAG (Ibrahim Index of African
Governance), 133, 136, 136*t*
Illiteracy, 10, 114

ILO (International Labour Organization), 115

IMIDSS (Integrated Medical Information and Disease Surveillance System), India, 104

Inclusiveness, as democratic aspect of good governance, 6, 42, 142, 145, 150

Income, 136, 149*t*
inequality of, and violence, 138, 143
MPI and, compared by country, 134*t*–135*t*
MPI as alternative poverty measurement, 113–115
as poverty measurement, 9, 111, 132

Index of Economic Freedom (IEF)
annual, from Heritage Foundation and Wall Street Journal, 57–58, 86*n*8
in CEE compared to FSU countries, 75–76, 77*f*

India, 106, 144, 147
education quality in, 94–95, 102–103
health care money in, 8, 97
health providers' absenteeism and training in, 97–98, 104
MPI and income poverty for, 135*t*

Indonesia, MPI and income poverty for, 134*t*

Institutions, 46, 146
building effective, for good governance, 142–147, 151–152
corruption in, and cultural factors, 59, 62–63, 84
responsive, and needs of citizenry, 132, 151

Integrated Medical Information and Disease Surveillance System (IMIDSS), biometric monitoring, 104

International assistance
economic development and, 148–149, 149*t*
prerequisites for, 52, 54, 86*n*2, 149
quality of governance and, 84–85, 145

International Classification of Diseases, Code Z59.5 in, 114

International Labour Organization (ILO), child laborers tracked by, 115

International Monetary Fund, IEF and, 58

Investment, 139
diaspora populations and, 147–148
redevelopment of transition economies and, 52, 86*nn*3–4
uncoordinated, and poverty traps, 116–117, 149

Iran, unrest in, 5, 146

Italy, political stability in, 46

Japan, property rights in, 147

Jinping, Pres. Xi, China, 151

Job creation, economic accountability and, 150

Job skills
diaspora populations and, 147–148
underpinned by uncoordinated investment, 117, 138

Kazakhstan, 134*t*
as an FSU country, 7, 86*n*12
corruption in, 64*f*, 76*f*
governance measures in, 66*f*, 68*f*, 70*f*, 72*f*, 73*f*, 77*f*

Kenya, 124
education in, 8, 106
governance and poverty measures compared for, 133, 135*t*, 136, 136*t*, 137*t*

Kickbacks. *See* Corruption

Korean peoples, governance of, 11, 152

Kosovo, 7, 76*f*, 86*n*13

Kyrgyz Republic, IEF in, 77*f*

Kyrgyzstan, 54
as an FSU country, 7, 86*n*12
corruption in, 64*f*, 76*f*
governance measures in, 66*f*, 68*f*, 70*f*, 72*f*, 73*f*

Laos, MPI and income poverty for, 134*t*

Latin America, 149*t*, 152
See also names of individual states, e.g., Bolivia

Latvia, 74
corruption in, 64f, 75, 76f
Latvia,
as either a CEE or FSU country, 7, 86n12
governance measures in, 66f, 68f, 70f, 71, 72f, 73f, 77f
LEA (Local educational agencies), 24, 25
Leadership challenges in developing countries, 10–13, 137, 152
Ethiopia in particular, 12, 145–147, 148
Legatum Index, core components of, 149
Legislators, hierarchical relationships in governance model and, 20, 24
Lesotho, IIAG scores for, 136, 137t
Liberal democracy, 143–144
Liberia, 145, 149
IIAG scores for, 136, 137t
Life in Transition Survey, corruption experiences reported in, 86n11
Light, Paul, 16
Lithuania, 74
corruption in, 64f, 75, 76f
as either a CEE or FSU country, 7, 86n12
governance measures in, 66f, 68f, 70f, 71, 72f, 73f, 77f
Local educational agencies (LEA), public education and, 24, 25
Los Angeles, California, value-added teacher performance measures in, 26–27

Macedonia
as a CEE country, 7, 86n13
corruption in, 64f, 76f
governance measures in, 67f, 69f, 70f, 72f, 74f, 77f
Madagascar, governance and poverty scores for, 135t, 136, 137t
Malawi, governance in, 136, 137t, 144
Malaysia, multiethnicity and majority rule in, 144
Mali
IIAG scores for, 136, 137t
preventable mortality in, 10, 114

Malthusian traps, fertility and, 117, 138
Mariam, Col. Mengistu Haile, 146
Mauritania, IIAG scores for, 136, 137t
Mauritius, governance in, 131, 136, 137t
MDGs (Millennium Development Goals), 9, 112
Measurement systems, 5, 10, 132
accountability, with CPI and FHI, 6, 7
governance and, 6, 39–40, 55–58, 131, 149
lessons in effectiveness improvements of, 17, 27–30
poverty, 11, 113–115, 132
student progress, 25, 28, 99, 102–103
value-added, for teacher performance, 26–27
Mexico, MPI and income poverty for, 134t
Middle East, 149t, 152
See also names of individual countries, e.g., Iran
Migration
climate migrants, 123, 125
foreign education of immigrants, 94–95
human development migrants, 144, 147–148
Military juntas, 140, 148
Millennium Development Goals (MDGs), as U.N. outline, 9, 112
Moldova
as an FSU country, 7, 86n12
corruption in, 64f, 76f
governance measures in, 66f, 68f, 70f, 72f, 73f, 77f
Montenegro, 76f, 77f
as a CEE country, 7, 86n13
Moral hazard, agency theory and, 18
Morsi, Pres. Mohamed, Egypt, 5, 146
Mortality rates, in developing countries, 10, 94, 114
Moynihan, Donald, 15–16
Mozambique, governance in, 136, 137t, 144
MPI. See Multidimensional Poverty Index

166 Asefa and Huang

Mubarak, Pres. Hosni, Egypt, 5
Mugabe, Robert, 145
Multidimensional Poverty Index (MPI),
  11, 133–136
  characteristics tracked by, 113–115
  compared to CPI, HDI, IIAG for
    selected African countries, 133,
    136*t*
  income and, compared by country,
    134*t*–135*t*
Myrdal, Gunnar, 116, 138

Namibia, IIAG scores for, 136, 137*t*
"Nation at Risk, A" (report), U.S.
  education in, 3–4, 23
Natural resources
  conflicts over, 124, 145
  depletion of, and poverty, 9, 10, 118,
    119, 139–140
  development potential of, 12–13, 144,
    147
  effect of climate change on, 121, 124
NCLB. *See* No Child Left Behind Act
  (2001)
NEPAD (New Partnership for Africa's
  Development), 125
Nepal, 98–99, 135*t*
New Partnership for Africa's
  Development (NEPAD),
  governance improvement of
  individual countries and, 125
New York (City), Dept. of Education,
  26, 28
New York (State), regional education-
  service centers in, 23–24
NGOs (Nongovernmental organizations),
  56, 147
Nicaragua, MPI and income poverty for,
  134*t*
Niger
  IIAG scores for, 136, 137*t*
  MPI and income poverty for, 133, 135*t*
  preventable mortality in, 10, 114
Nigeria, 136*t*
  conflict vulnerability in, 138–139

conflicts over natural resources in,
  124, 145
education in, *vs.* France and dollar
  value, 94–95
IIAG scores for, 136, 137*t*
No Child Left Behind Act (NCLB,
  2001), 24
  linear improvement expectations of,
    18–19, 19*f*
  standardized testing in, and
    educational success, 3, 22, 25–26
Nokomo, Joshua, 145
Nongovernmental organizations (NGOs),
  offices of, 56, 147
Nordic states. *See* Denmark; Norway;
  Sweden
North Korea, governance of, 11, 152
Norway, high standard of governance
  in, 131
Nutrition
  mal-, as poverty trap, 10, 114, 132
  under-, and workforce energy, 113,
    117, 139

Obama, Pres. Barack, U.S., 4, 143
Obamacare. *See* Patient Protection and
  Affordable Care Act (2010)
Ohio, regional education-service centers
  in, 23–24
Organizational authority, hierarchical
  relationships in governance model
  and, 20–21, 24
Oslo Peace Research Institute, cyclic
  projections by, 138
Ottoman Empire, collapse of, 11

Pahlavi, Shah Mohammad Reza, Iran, 5
Pakistan, MPI and income poverty for,
  134*t*
Patient Protection and Affordable Care
  Act (2010), multiple goals and
  conflicting objectives of, 2, 20–21
Peace, 131, 138, 151
Pedersen's Index, electoral volatility
  and, 41

Performance-based contracts, 17
  complexities in establishment of, 18, 21
  market-based incentives in, 21–22
  service delivery with, and agency theory, 2–3
Performance management, 8
  blunt application of, in public sector, 17, 23–27
  complexities of, in public sector, 20–22
  diagnostic tools for, 3, 27, 29
  lessons in effectiveness improvements of, 17, 27–30
  origins of, 16, 17–19, 25–26
  public education and, 3–4, 18
  role of, in good governance, 2–3, 15–17
  unintended consequences of, 21–22, 27
Poland, 59
  as a CEE country, 7, 86*n*13
  corruption in, 64*f,* 76*f*
  governance measures in, 67*f,* 69*f,* 70*f,* 72*f,* 74*f,* 77*f*
Political authority, governance and, 1, 6, 7
Political freedom, 150, 151
Political influence, public *vs.* private sector and, 22, 26
Political parties
  corruption and, 4, 35, 36, 37, 38, 40, 45
  definitions of, 41, 47*n*1
  fragmentation (number) of, 37–41, 43*t,* 44, 44*t,* 45*t,* 47*n*2, 145
  functions performed by, 35–36, 36*t*
  influence of, on democracy in developing countries, 4–6, 35–37
  institutionalized aspects of, 37–38, 40, 142
  one-party dominance, 4, 37, 38, 39, 41, 43*t,* 44, 44*t,* 45*t,* 145, 146, 150
  study of good governance with, 39–47, 145

  study results and conclusion about, 42–47
  volatility of, 38, 40–41, 43*t,* 44, 44*t,* 45*t*
Political rights, 144
  Freedom House survey of, 57, 74
  as governance measurement, 6, 75*f*
Political stability, 7
  as aspect of good governance, 1, 5, 6, 46–47, 57, 87*n*23, 131
  in CEE compared to FSU countries, 71, 73*f,* 74
  as dependent study variable, 40, 41, 43
  post–civil war states, 44, 45*t*
Poverty
  addressing, traps, 10, 11, 116–118, 137–138
  addressing, with good governance, 13, 115–116, 119
  environmental degradation and, 111, 112, 118
  multiple dimensions of, 11, 113–115
  natural resources depletion and, 9, 10, 112
  poor governance as driver of, 11, 138–140
  U.N. and, 9–10
Poverty reduction, 150
  35 years of recent progress toward, 111–112
  challenges and constraints on, 111, 115, 118–122
  climate change and, 8–10
  good governance and, 4, 115–116, 125–126, 131, 136, 152
Private sector, 111
  corrupt "state capture" in, 5, 58, 65, 76, 87*nn*16–17
Property rights, 124
  land ownership and reform, 138, 140, 146–147
  rules for, from effective and inclusive institutions, 142, 147
Public education, 26, 30
  chaotic governing structures in, 23–25

Public education, *cont.*
  gaming the system, 18, 22, 27, 103
  quality of, and economic progress, 3–4
  students ill-served by, 19, 25
Public policy, 7
  aligning employment goals with, 3, 150
  implementation of, and governance, 1, 85, 122–126
  planned adaptation in, 122–125
Public sector, 15, 111
  administration of, and reform movements, 16, 17
  blunt applications of performance management in, 17, 23–27
  child welfare systems in, 2, 21–22
  complexities of performance management in, 16, 20–22, 30
  corrupt "grabbing hand" in, 58, 65, 87nn16–17
  policing in, and effective performance management data, 29–30
  political influence on, and changing priorities, 22, 30n2
Public sector agencies, 131
  hierarchical relationships in governance model and, 20–21, 24
  service quality by, and obstacles to business, 77–78, 88n24, 88n26

Rape, as violent weapon, 120
Reagan, Pres. Ronald, U.S., 30n2
Refugees, 120, 145
Regional cooperation, 23–24, 147–149
Regulatory quality
  as aspect of good governance, 1, 6, 54, 57, 87n22, 131
  CEE *vs.* FSU scores in, 60, 61f, 62, 65, 67f, 68
  permit applications in CEE compared to FSU countries, 80, 82f, 83f, 85f
  time taxes in, 7, 80, 82f
Religious conflict, 143, 145
  Boko Haram in Nigeria and, 138–139
  exclusivity and, 5, 6, 146

Rent seeking, as form of corruption, 140–141, 142
Revolutionary democracy, as misnomer, 143
Rhodesia, postcolonial. *See* Zimbabwe
Robinson, James A., coauthor of *Why Nations Fail*, 11, 152
Roman Empire, collapse of, 11
Romania
  as a CEE country, 7, 86n13
  corruption in, 64f, 76f
  governance measures in, 67f, 69f, 70f, 72f, 74f, 77f
Roosevelt, Pres. Theodore, U.S., 148
Rosenstein-Rodan, Paul, 116–117
Rule of law
  as aspect of good governance, 1, 6, 12, 53, 57, 131, 132
  from effective and inclusive institutions, 142, 147
  measurements of, 7, 133
  in selected countries, 68, 69f, 71, 150
Rural areas, 102, 116, 123
  facilities and services in, 98, 100
Russia
  as an FSU country, 7, 86n12
  corruption in, 62, 64f, 65, 76f, 87n20
  culture of kinship and reciprocity in, 59, 63
  governance measures in, 66f, 68f, 70f, 72f, 73f, 77f
Russian Federation, one-party dominance in, 42
Rwanda, IIAG scores for, 136, 137t

Safety, 139
  as component of governance indexes, 133, 149
  social, nets, 51, 54, 142
São Tomé and Príncipe, IIAG scores for, 136, 137t
Scholarly opinion, political parties and, 4
Scientific management movement, 16, 25
  monitoring of workforce in, 17–18, 103
SEA (State educational agencies), 24, 25

Sen, Amartya K., 144
Senegal, governance in, 131, 136, 137*t*, 144
Serbia
    as a CEE country, 7, 86*n*13
    corruption in, 64*f*, 76*f*
    governance measures in, 67*f*, 69*f*, 70*f*, 72*f*, 74*f*, 77*f*
Seychelles, IIAG scores for, 136, 137*t*
Sierra Leone, 145
    IIAG scores for, 136, 137*t*
    preventable mortality in, 10, 114
Skills, low as poverty trap, 10, 117
Slavery, 115, 139, 143
Slovakia
    as a CEE country, 7, 86*n*13
    corruption in, 64*f*, 76*f*
    governance measures in, 67*f*, 69*f*, 70*f*, 72*f*, 74*f*, 77*f*
Slovenia
    as a CEE country, 7, 86*n*13
    corruption in, 64*f*, 76*f*
    governance measures in, 67*f*, 69*f*, 70*f*, 72*f*, 74*f*, 77*f*
Social capital, 149
    development of, 1, 51
    kinship and reciprocity as, 59, 62–63, 84
Social democracy, requirements of, 143
Social service agencies, 21, 61, 120
    child welfare among, 2–3
    safety nets and, 51, 54
Somalia, 147
    governance and poverty measures compared for selected African countries, 133, 136*t*
    IIAG scores for, 136, 137*t*
South Africa, 144, 145
    apartheid's collapse in, 142–143
    IIAG scores for, 136, 137*t*
South Korea, 147
    governance of, contrasted with North Korea, 11, 152
Soviet Union, collapse of, 6–7, 11, 143, 148

Standard of Living, as human development measurement, 132, 133
State educational agencies (SEA), public education and, 24, 25
Sudan
    conflicts over natural resources in, 123, 145
    governance and poverty measures compared for, 136*t*
    IIAG scores for, 136, 137*t*
Sustainable economic development, 4, 136
    China and, 12, 112
    relationships of, to governance and MPI, 11, 136–137
    requirements of, 1, 51
Swaziland, IIAG scores for, 136, 137*t*
Sweden, high standard of governance in, 131, 143

Taiwan, property rights in, 147
Tajikistan
    as an FSU country, 7, 86*n*12
    corruption in, 64*f*, 76*f*
    governance measures in, 66*f*, 68*f*, 70*f*, 72*f*, 73*f*, 77*f*
Tanzania, 136*t*, 144
    IIAG scores for, 136, 137*t*
    MPI and income poverty for, 133, 135*t*
Taxes, 101
    corruption's effect on, 61, 87*n*20
    regulation of, in CEE compared to FSU countries, 7, 80, 82*f*
Taylor, Frederick, 25
Teachers
    incentive schemes for, 99, 102–103
    value-added performance measures for, 26, 27
Texas, regional education-service centers in, 23–24
Thailand, MPI and income poverty for, 134*t*
Third Plenum, governance reform and, 12, 151
Tides of Reform, The (Light), 16

Time taxes, bureaucracy and, 7, 80, 82*f*

Tito, Josip Broz, 143

Togo, IIAG scores for, 136, 137*t*

Trade, quality of governance and, 138, 147

Trade-offs, simple *vs.* complicated systems and, 18, 28

Transition economies, 51
business firms' perspective on, 6, 7, 76–83
CEE countries with, 6–7
comparing, on good governance, 58–76
ethnicity in study of, 42, 43*t,* 44*t,* 45*t*
FSU countries with, 6–7
good governance in, for economic development, 51–55, 83–88, 86*nn*1–4
good governance measures in, 55–58, 86*nn*6–11
WGIs of former socialist countries with, 33, 56–57, 60, 61*f,* 86*n*5

Transparency, 29, 133
as aspect of good governance, 6, 53, 132, 132*t*

Transparency International (organization), CPI produced by, 6, 57

Turkmenistan
as an FSU country, 7, 86*n*12
corruption in, 64*f,* 76*f*
governance measures in, 68*f,* 70*f,* 72*f,* 73*f,* 77*f*

Uganda, 136*t*
citizen empowerment in, 8, 104–105, 106
education money in, 7–8
graft in, 96–97
IIAG scores for, 136, 137*t*

Ukraine
as an FSU country, 7, 86*n*12
corruption in, 64*f,* 76*f*
governance measures in, 68*f,* 70*f,* 72*f,* 73*f,* 77*f*

UNDP (U.N. Development Programme), 113–114

United Nations (U.N.), 9, 147
organizations within, 114, 115
poverty and, 9–10
UNDP of, and MPI, 113–114

United States (U.S.)
international relations and, 148, 149*t,* 152
K–12 education in, 3–4, 23

U.S. Agency for International Development (USAID),new democracies and, 46

U.S. Congress, Senate, committee testimonies, 19

U.S. Dept. of Education, 18–19, 24

U.S. Environmental Protection Agency (EPA), changed agency priorities of, 30–31*n*2

U.S. law and legislation
education, 3, 18–19, 24
health care, 2, 20–21

U.S. Peace Corps, 148

USAID (U.S. Agency for International Development), 46

Uzbekistan
as an FSU country, 7, 86*n*12
control of corruption in, 64*f*
governance measures in, 67*f,* 68*f,* 70*f,* 72*f,* 73*f,* 77*f*

Vietnam, MPI and income poverty for, 134*t*

Violence
absence of, as aspect of good governance, 1, 87*n*23, 131
civil wars and, 42, 43, 44, 138
climate-driven conflict and, 9, 111, 121
effects on noncombatants, 119–120
governments overthrown by, 5, 46, 146
income inequality and, 138, 143

Voice, 116
free press as, 144, 150

Index   171

Voice, *cont.*
  government repression of, 144, 145, 152
  paired with accountability as aspect of good governance, 1, 57, 60, 61*f,* 71, 71*f,* 87*n*14, 131, 150

Wages, 123
  low, as performance factor, 8, 100
  supplemental bonuses to, and unintended effects, 21–22, 29, 99
Washington, Pres. George, U.S.
  opinion of, about political parties, 4, 35
Washington consensus, economic growth and, 54
Wayne County, Michigan, child welfare agencies in, 2, 21–22
Welfare-to-work programs, performance management and, 28
WFO (World Food Organization), 114
WGIs. *See* Worldwide Governance Indicators
Why Nations Fail (Acemoglu and Robinson), 11, 152
Wilson, Woodrow, 16
Women, 8, 139
  effects of poverty on, 10, 114
  role of, in Egyptian society, 5, 146
Workforce, 16, 28
  absenteeism and shirking as governance problems, 97–98, 102
  energy of, and undernutrition, 117, 139
  monitoring of, actions and outcomes, 17–18, 100–101, 103–104
  performance and training of, 8, 98
  principled actions by, and employing agencies, 2–3, 30–31*n*2
World Bank
  good governance according to, 1, 39–40, 47, 53
  (*see also* Worldwide Governance Indicators [WGIs])
  political data banks provided by, 5, 39
  reports by, 9, 58, 112

  rules-based *vs.* outcome measures and, 55–56
World Food Organization (WFO), global hunger and malnutrition tracking by, 114
Worldwide Governance Indicators (WGIs), 131
  core components of, 56–57, 86*n*5, 87*nn*14–15, 87*nn*21–23, 131
  former socialist countries and, 7, 56, 59, 60, 86*nn*11–12
  scores for CEE compared to FSU countries, 60, 61*f,* 63*f,* 66*f,* 67*f,* 69*f,* 71*f,* 73*f*

Yemen, MPI and income poverty for, 134*t*
Yugoslavia, 59, 143

Zambia, IIAG scores for, 136, 137*t*
ZANU (Zimbabwe African National Union) party, 145
Zimbabwe, 145
  contrasted with other African countries, 11, 149
  IIAG scores for, 136, 137*t*
  MPI and income poverty for, 133, 134*t*

About the Institute

The W.E. Upjohn Institute for Employment Research is a nonprofit research organization devoted to finding and promoting solutions to employment-related problems at the national, state, and local levels. It is an activity of the W.E. Upjohn Unemployment Trustee Corporation, which was established in 1932 to administer a fund set aside by Dr. W.E. Upjohn, founder of The Upjohn Company, to seek ways to counteract the loss of employment income during economic downturns.

The Institute is funded largely by income from the W.E. Upjohn Unemployment Trust, supplemented by outside grants, contracts, and sales of publications. Activities of the Institute comprise the following elements: 1) a research program conducted by a resident staff of professional social scientists; 2) a competitive grant program, which expands and complements the internal research program by providing financial support to researchers outside the Institute; 3) a publications program, which provides the major vehicle for disseminating the research of staff and grantees, as well as other selected works in the field; and 4) an Employment Management Services division, which manages most of the publicly funded employment and training programs in the local area.

The broad objectives of the Institute's research, grant, and publication programs are to 1) promote scholarship and experimentation on issues of public and private employment and unemployment policy, and 2) make knowledge and scholarship relevant and useful to policymakers in their pursuit of solutions to employment and unemployment problems.

Current areas of concentration for these programs include causes, consequences, and measures to alleviate unemployment; social insurance and income maintenance programs; compensation; workforce quality; work arrangements; family labor issues; labor-management relations; and regional economic development and local labor markets.